# Faith Matters

# Faith Matters

*Reflections on the Christian Life*

## KERRY WALTERS

CASCADE *Books* • Eugene, Oregon

FAITH MATTERS
Reflections on the Christian Life

Copyright © 2019 Kerry Walters. All rights reserved. Except for brief quotations in critical publications or reviews, no part of this book may be reproduced in any manner without prior written permission from the publisher. Write: Permissions, Wipf and Stock Publishers, 199 W. 8th Ave., Suite 3, Eugene, OR 97401.

Cascade Books
An Imprint of Wipf and Stock Publishers
199 W. 8th Ave., Suite 3
Eugene, OR 97401

www.wipfandstock.com

PAPERBACK ISBN: 978-1-5326-7037-4
HARDCOVER ISBN: 978-1-5326-7038-1
EBOOK ISBN: 978-1-5326-7039-8

*Cataloguing-in-Publication data:*

Names: Walters, Kerry, author.

Title: Faith matters : reflections on the Christian life. / by Kerry Walters.

Description: Eugene, OR: Cascade Books, 2019.

Identifiers: ISBN 978-1-5326-7037-4 (paperback) | ISBN 978-1-5326-7038-1 (hardcover) | ISBN 978-1-5326-7039-8 (ebook)

Subjects: LCSH: Christian life. | Christianity.

Classification: BV4598.2 W15 2019 (paperback) | BV4598.2 (ebook)

Manufactured in the U.S.A.                             06/13/19

For Kim and Jonah

# Contents

Introduction | 1

## Part 1: This Christian Thing
Philosopher Jesus | 5
In Defense of Religion | 8
Biblical Illiteracy | 11
Stiff-Necked Christians | 14
Christian Mosaic | 17
Stripping Down | 20
Meeting the Enemy | 23
God-Wired | 26
Slaves and Masters | 28
Wedding Joy | 30

## Part 2: The Spiritual Life
Loneliness | 35
Zombies | 37
Original Blessing | 40
Gorged But Starving | 42
Kissing God | 44
God's Need for Love | 46
Becoming Prayer | 49
Divine *Nada* | 52
We Are God's Wombs | 54
Grace-Mobbed | 56

**Part 3: Being Good**
Nothing Is Permitted | 61
Capital Punishment Is a Sin | 63
Reclaiming Prudence | 65
Against Moral Relativism | 67
Getting Clear on Conscience | 69
Physician-Assisted Suicide | 71
Moral Imagination | 73
Rehabilitating Shame | 76
Doing What Thou Wilt | 78
Our Sex-Obsessed Prophets | 80

**Part 4: Culture and Community**
Weathering a New Dark Age | 85
All Sheep, No Goats | 88
Breathing in Hiroshima | 90
When Darkness Descends | 92
Whitewashing the Faith | 95
The Jesus Line | 98
Golden Rule Justice | 100
Democratizing Evil | 102
Christian Nation Basics | 105
Moral Distribution of Wealth | 108

**Part 5: All Saints**
Saint of the Gutter | 113
Serving Christ in Friends and Strangers | 115
In Praise of Erasmus | 118
Eye to Eye | 120
The Grand Experiment | 122
A Lesson from the Gulag | 125
He Got Christ Out of the Churches | 127
Oxford's Inklings | 129
The Dumb Ox | 132
A Sacrosanct Right | 135

**Part 6: Behold the Beauty**
Gauguin's Questions | 139
The Sistine Gem | 141
Like Anemones | 144
Hidden in Plain Sight | 147
Poetry is God's Language | 150
Naked Intent | 152
Luke's Icon | 154
The Real da Vinci Code | 156
Ragged Edges | 158
Starry Night, Golden Sun | 161

**Part 7: Mosaic of Beliefs**
The Scandal of Scientific Illiteracy | 167
Denying Evolution | 170
Fool's Gold | 173
Heart Knowledge | 175
Pretend Believers | 177
Double Standard | 179
Unintelligent Design | 181
Big Bang Boogie | 183
Searching for Common Ground | 186
When Science Oversteps | 188

**Part 8: To Everything There Is a Season**
Stretching Forward (Advent) | 193
The Great O's (Advent) | 195
They Who Are Wisest (Christmas) | 197
Yuletide Magic (Christmas) | 199
Rachel Weeping (Feast of the Holy Innocents) | 201
Soul Journey (Epiphany) | 204
Becoming Saints (Lent) | 207
The True Myth (Easter) | 210
Sign of the Phoenix (Easter) | 212
Light and Darkness (Feast of the Transfiguration) | 214

# Introduction

Does faith really matter? I think so. I hope so.

For several years now I've written a weekly newspaper column called "Faith Matters." The column's name, and the title of this collection of a few that my newspaper readers most liked, is a pretty obvious double entendre that gestures at both the contents of faith and its importance.

The two things I most want to avoid in offering these short reflections are syrupy, feel-good piety and preachy holier-than-thou judgmentalism. These days, there's way too much of that masquerading as Christianity. Instead, my aim is to encourage readers, both those who're already professed Christians and those indifferent or even hostile to Christianity, to go a bit more deeply into the nature and message of faith. As Saint Paul urged (1 Cor 14:20), all of us, believers and nonbelievers alike, should think about faith like adults, not children.

That's because the faith which we Christians profess and its cultured despisers reject is as smart and insightful as it is compassionate and kind. Too frequently, Christians reduce faith to feeling or emotion, and its critics to bigoted, willful ignorance. But both of these are caricatures. At its heart, faith is a kind of "big-picture" knowledge or worldview grounded in a particular relationship with God. This worldview has birthed some of the most stunningly brilliant works of art, philosophy, theology, and science—we too often forget this fourth area of Christian endeavor, by the way—in human history. Although the faith can be expressed in a couple of simple creeds inherited from the apostles and the Council of Nicaea, it's anything but simplistic.

"Faith," of course, is a multivalent word. Nothing is foreign to it. In these short reflections, I've paid due diligence to its richness by meditating on its relationship to the sciences and its need to dialogue with atheism; its ability to shed light upon our world and the Creator who uttered it (and us!)

into existence; the beauty that inspires faith and the goodness that flows from it; the social and cultural responsibilities which faith obliges us to take on; the ways in which we express faith in our everyday spiritualities; the saints whose examples of faith strengthen our own; and the seasons within the Christian calendar that invite us to explore different facets of faith.

The reflections gathered here have been grouped into eight categories that express faith's multivalence and also provide readers with a kind of topical roadmap. But there's no correct way to go about diving into them, and I'm not at all convinced that reading a book like this consecutively from start to finish is the best way to go. So feel free to let the titles on the contents page take you where they will.

And regardless of where you begin reading, remember: faith *does* matter.

Kerry Walters
Feast of Saint Francis of Assisi, 2018

# PART 1

# This Christian Thing

# Philosopher Jesus

As *praefectus urbi*, chief administrator of the imperial city of Rome, Junius Bassus was an important man in his day. But he would be entirely forgotten—such is the ephemerality of fame—were it not for his death.

Bassus died in AD 359 at the youngish age, even for fourth-century Rome, of forty-two. Befitting his high office, he was entombed in an elaborately sculpted sarcophagus. We know that he was a Christian because the front of his sarcophagus is decorated with ten relief panels depicting scenes from the Hebrew and Christian Scriptures.

Bassus's tomb is one of the earliest extant pieces of Christian relief sculpture. It's not remarkable as an *objet d'art*; the carved figures' heads are too big for their rather squat, gravity-burdened bodies. The real value of the sarcophagus is what it tells us about how fourth-century Romans looked at Jesus.

By the time of Bassus's death, Christianity was only just being integrated into the Roman Empire. Constantine the Great had ended the persecution of Christians a mere generation earlier, and mid-fourth-century Christian Romans were still trying to wrap their minds around the notion of a Hebraic God-man. It was inevitable that their interpretation of Christianity took on elements from existing paganism, and this hybridization is obvious in the centerpiece relief of Bassus's sarcophagus.

In it, Jesus is seated, with the apostles Peter and Paul standing on either side of him. Jesus's feet rest on a mythological figure of indeterminate identity, but is probably Aeolus, god of the winds. There's nothing out of the ordinary thus far. Peter and Paul are the two chief apostles of the new religion, and Jesus's trampling of Aeolus probably synthesizes his victory over the old gods.

Part 1: This Christian Thing

But a couple of other details startle our twenty-first-century Christian sensibilities. The first is that Jesus is depicted as a beardless youth. The second is that he holds a scroll in his left hand. (His right hand is missing.) It's tempting to imagine the scroll as a symbol of the gospel. But that would be a mistake, because Jesus is clothed in the easily recognizable toga of a classical philosopher. And just to make sure the point isn't missed, the sculptor, in another panel, places the traditional staff of an itinerant philosopher in Jesus's hand.

The Jesus depicted on Bassus's sarcophagus is, despite his youth, a sage, a lover of wisdom. He's a philosopher. This is surprising enough. But just as striking is the absence on the sarcophagus of any overt statement of Jesus's divinity. The only indication is a curiously reticent one: the symbolic trampling of Aeolus.

It's as if Bassus's tomb loudly proclaims that Jesus is a great moral teacher, the latest in a distinguished line of Hellenistic philosophers, but then, in a comparatively muted aside, adds the possibility that he might also be God.[1]

In his 2008 encyclical *Spe Salvi*, Benedict XVI suggested that Jesus is depicted as a philosopher because the ancient meaning of the word denoted a person who teaches how to be "authentically human."[2] As the new Adam and new Eve, Jesus demonstrates in word and deed what God means humans to be. It's a fresh revelation, symbolized on the sarcophagus by Jesus's youth, of the ancient wisdom lost through the fall of our primordial parents, Eve and Adam.

Perhaps. But I think another explanation is that the Christ-event mystified fourth-century Romans, and that just as Christian theology at the time used existing Greek and Roman philosophical categories to make sense of God, so popular piety somewhat confusedly melded Jesus and itinerant sages.

The truth is that every generation and every culture is mystified by the Christ—a point conceded in John's Gospel when he writes that there aren't enough books in the world to capture the meaning of Jesus—and so each inevitably tries to make some sense of him by falling back on familiarly conventional categories. You and I may find Bassus's philosopher Jesus

---

1. Interested readers may view an image of Bassus's tomb here: Riley Winters, "The Sarcophagus of Junius Bassus: How a Coffin Defeated the Gods," https://www.ancient-origins.net/artifacts-other-artifacts/sarcophagus-junius-bassus-how-coffin-defeated-gods-008823.

2. Pope Benedict XVI, *Spe Salvi* (San Francisco: Ignatius, 2008), 18.

spiritually anemic. But two millennia from now, our own way of looking at Jesus may seem equally odd to our descendants.

Skeptics might say that this ever-evolving interpretation of Jesus points to the make-it-up-as-you-go nature of Christianity. But I think that the many masks Jesus has worn throughout the centuries simply acknowledges that the ever-present God is also ever-elusive. To we who see only darkly, how could it be otherwise?

# In Defense of Religion

"I'm spiritual, not religious."

We hear this everywhere these days, particularly from millennials. In fact, 47 percent of the one-fifth of adults in this country who are religiously unaffiliated say it.[1]

Spiritual-not-religiousers typically aren't very specific when it comes to explaining what they mean by "spiritual." They most often appeal to a rather vague belief in a transcendent reality of some sort or a diffuse sense of awe at the majesty of the cosmos.

They're much clearer about what they mean by "religious." For them, the word refers to "institutionalized" faith traditions which, they contend, demand unwavering acceptance of certain tenets, prescribe narrow codes of conduct, and are larded with ritualistic rigmarole. They believe that religion as practiced in churches, temples, and mosques enchains the mind with formulaic doctrine, burdens life with joylessly puritanical norms, and belabors the spirit with incomprehensible liturgy.

I get and even partly sympathize with the point spiritual-not-religiousers wish to make. No honest religionist can deny that religious institutions are capable of spiritual atrophy, arrogant intolerance, arcane ritualism, and heartbreaking scandal. Institutions, religious or otherwise, are human artifacts, and thus always susceptible to corruption.

Still, despite the fact that religion can go bad, I'm unwilling to throw it over for the sake of an amorphous spirituality. Embedded within religion at its best is a depth and richness that's folded into the word's very meaning.

The English word "religion" is derived from the Latin *religio*, which for the ancient Romans denoted ritualistic obligations to God. But etymologists

---

[1]. Pew Research Center, "More Americans Now Say They're Spiritual but Not Religious," https://www.pewresearch.org/fact-tank/2017/09/06/more-americans-now-say-theyre-spiritual-but-not-religious/, Table 5.

are split over *religio's* roots, debating whether it derives from *relegere* or *religare*.

The pagan philosopher Cicero favored *relegere*, which means to ponder, examine, or peruse. The Christian theologian Augustine, on the other hand, plunked down for *religare*: to bind, fasten, or tie together.

Although a lot of ink has been spilt since Cicero's and Augustine's day on this etymological debate, it seems to me that religion in its most authentic form is a marriage of both *relegere* and *religare*. Recognizing this might make spiritual-not-religiousers a bit less dismissive of religion, and religionists a bit more appreciative of the inner meaning of their traditions.

The *relegere* dimension of authentic religion invites us to ponder the wonderment that fills us when we contemplate the starry heavens above and the moral law within. Why is there something rather than nothing? Why am I here? What kind of person ought I to be? These are the core musings that fuel religion. They impel us to dare to dive below life's shallows, plumb its depths, and draw ever nearer to the Divine Mystery.

Religious creeds, which spiritual-not-religiousers dismiss as inflexible dogmas, are efforts to express our human ponderings about the universe and the God who created it. They don't pretend to be exhaustive. How could words ever capture the ultimately unknowable essence of God? They are, instead, guideposts.

Creedal ponderings are essential aspects of authentic religion, but they're not sufficient. The human soul isn't just curious about God and God's work. It also yearns for total, unqualified connection with the divine Source that pulsates at reality's core. As Augustine said, our hearts are achingly restless until we rest in the God of love. Otherwise, we're incomplete.

This is where the *religare* dimension of religion comes in. Authentic religion facilitates the loving connection with God that we crave. Although distrusted by spiritual-not-religiousers, religious rituals tie us to God by reminding us in concrete, lived ways of God's abiding presence in our lives. They help us bind ourselves ever more closely to the God who, in turn, gladly offers himself to us.

The *religare* dimension of religion also clues us into the all-important fact that our ultimate fulfillment requires a loving connection, not just to God, but to the entire community of believers as well.

Spirituality-not-religion is often radically individualistic. Religion never is. It keeps us mindful that we're children of a common Parent who loves us all equally. We're bound by the deepest of familial ties to one another and to God, a fact acknowledged whenever we worship together. Religious moral codes, which spiritual-not-religiousers see as stultifying, are efforts, subject to continuous pondering, to help us honor our connectedness by loving one another as God loves us.

So, to my spiritual-not-religiouser friends, peace be with you on your journey. I wish you Godspeed, and I'm sure our paths will occasionally cross.

But I'll stick with religion.

# Biblical Illiteracy

Time for a pop quiz. Which of the following phrases are found in the Old Testament, and which in the New?

*God helps those who help themselves.*

*Spare the rod and spoil the child.*

*Cleanliness is next to godliness.*

*God works in mysterious ways.*

*Hate the sin, love the sinner.*

This is a trick question, because even though these expressions often are given a biblical pedigree, not one of them actually appears in Scripture. If you thought otherwise, you're not alone. Despite all the Bible-thumping that goes on in this country, biblical illiteracy is widespread. The Good Book is one of those classics more often invoked than read.

Data from the Barna Group, a Christian polling firm, show that 58 percent of us claim that the Bible is the literal or inspired word of God, and a whopping 87 percent of households own at least one Bible. No surprises there.[1]

When it comes to actually reading all those Good Books, however, the numbers plummet. Although 37 percent of Americans report reading the Bible once a week or more,[2] most glance at Scripture only four times a year, typically during holidays like Easter or Christmas. Americans are so unversed in the book more than half of us claim to revere that we confuse

---

1. Barna Group, "State of the Bible 2017: Top Findings," https://www.barna.com/research/state-bible-2017-top-findings/.

2. Alec Gallup and Wendy W. Simmons, "Six in Ten Americans Read Bible at Least Occasionally," *Gallup News*, October 20, 2000, https://news.gallup.com/poll/2416/six-ten-americans-read-bible-least-occasionally.aspx, para. 1.

## Part 1: This Christian Thing

the Hebraic King Saul with the apostle Saul/Paul, conclude that Joan of Arc is Noah's wife, believe that Sodom and Gomorrah are a married couple, and think that the Sermon on the Mount was preached by Billy Graham.

These are real examples, by the way. You can't make this stuff up.

Only 45 percent of respondents can name the four Gospels in order, an exercise you'd think would be about as minimally taxing as naming the first four presidents. America, concludes pollster George Barna, is in "a crisis of biblical illiteracy."

It gets worse. Not only do Christians not know their Bible, they're also not particularly up on what their denominations profess. According to a 2010 Pew survey, 45 percent of Catholics are unaware that their tradition holds that communion bread and wine transubstantiate into Christ's body and blood. Protestants shouldn't feel smarter, however, because a full 53 percent of them have no idea who Martin Luther was. Nearly half of all Christians admit to never reading religious books of any kind.

The worst offenders turn out to be white mainline Protestants and Catholics. When quizzed about Christianity and world religions, they scored lower than Mormons, evangelical white Protestants, black Protestants, and Jews. And get this: they were also bested by atheists and agnostics.

What accounts for this astounding illiteracy? A significant factor has got to be the proliferation of nominal Christians, people who inherit a religious affiliation but have no real commitment to it and even less curiosity about it. It's not that they're hostile to Christianity. They're just indifferent. Inertia may keep some of them in the pews, but they're yawningly bored by the white-bread answers rotely trotted out to questions they don't even care enough to ask. What possible incentive could they have for reading the Bible or learning more about the faith?

The truth—disturbing to some, welcomed by others—is that the same indifference to Christianity that's already overtaken Europe is seeping into America. The United States still comes across as an intensely religious nation, largely because Protestant evangelicals, whose numbers are slipping, are so noisy. But let's be honest: much of what passes for Christianity in this country is more cultural artifact than living commitment.

The proper response to biblical illiteracy isn't a panicky handing out of yet more Bibles on street corners, but doing something about the indifference that breeds it. Mainline churches are being called to do some serious soul-searching about how to proclaim and live the gospel authentically in an increasingly post-Christian America. For believers, the word of God is eternal. But the perennial challenge for faith communities is to communicate that word in ways that speak to each new generation. That we're becoming a nation of religious illiterates testifies to the unhappy fact that the ball has been dropped. If American Christianity hopes to make it through the wintry season it's entering, it has to reignite fire in the belly, hope in the heart, and curiosity in the mind.

And that just might spell the end of the church as we know it. To paraphrase a passage that really is in Scripture, the kernel must die to produce fruit.

# Stiff-Necked Christians

The Hebrew prophets didn't mince words. Whenever they saw their countrymen falling into religious hypocrisy, moral indifference, and judgmental self-righteousness, they chastised them in no uncertain terms.

The most common epithets the prophets hurled at sinners were "idolaters," "betrayers," "thieves," "faithless," and "cursed." What each of these offenses had in common was a spiritual perversity that the prophets referred to as *qesheh ʿoreph*. The expression literally means "hard of neck," typically translated in the Bible as "stiff-necked."

*Qesheh ʿoreph* was originally a husbandry term referring to an ox that stubbornly resisted pulling a harrow or plow in a straight line. When applied to humans, it came to designate dismal qualities like obstinacy, rebelliousness, hypocrisy, and overreaching pride.

To be called a "stiff-necked people" was a terrible indictment, implying as it did that the sacred covenant with Yahweh had been betrayed by a society too intent on pursuing its own interests to bother with God.

It's a funny thing. Whenever we Christians read the prophets and apply their denunciations to our own day, our tendency is nearly always to assume that they're directed at others and never ourselves. *We're* good, decent people. It's *them*, those wicked *others*, who the prophets are calling out. They're the stiff-necked ones.

But what we American Christians need to come to terms with is that the prophets are speaking directly to us. Their accusing fingers point straight at our sins, and we richly deserve their harshest rebukes. For we're in danger of becoming a stiff-necked people, quick to judge and condemn others, and equally quick to preen ourselves on what we consider to be our rectitude.

Why do I say this? Just consider our toxic abuses of the faith in recent years. Not every American Christian is guilty of them, of course. I

## Stiff-Necked Christians

personally know women and men whose personal saintliness humbles and inspires me. But too frequently, the rancor that increasingly infects our culture trickles down to our churches. Frequently, it does so through our religious leaders, especially those who lust after the golden ring of celebrityhood.

We American Christians are a stiff-necked people whenever:

- we use the faith as a bludgeon to hector, bully, and condemn gays, foreigners, Muslims, women, liberals, conservatives, persons of color, the poor, the rich, fellow Christians who belong to denominations other than our own, and anyone else we don't like;
- we focus obsessively on sin and damnation, showing little compassion for human weaknesses (except, of course, our own);
- we justify our vitriol by pretending it's "godly indignation";
- we defend our intractability by calling it "faith";
- we live two separate existences: a pious, platitude-mouthing one on Sunday mornings, and a cutthroat, me-centered one the rest of the week;
- we swat at moral gnats but swallow entire camels, privileging isolated and arcane biblical passages that proscribe certain kinds of private behavior while giving a thumbs-up to legal, social, and economic institutions that benefit *us* but oppress *them*;
- we sideline the spirit of love, compassion, and non-judgmentalism practiced and taught by Jesus in favor of competition, censure, and criticism;
- we look down our noses at others and, like the arrogant Pharisee in Luke's Gospel, arrogantly thank God we are not like *them*;
- we refuse to recognize that an action or kind of behavior isn't necessarily immoral simply because we personally disapprove of it or find it distasteful;
- we conflate our political positions with our religious ones, no matter how contrary to the gospel our political stands might be;
- we sputter at the least provocation that our religious freedom is being violated, all the while remaining silently indifferent to the real life-and-death persecution of Christians in other parts of the world.

## Part 1: This Christian Thing

Jesus warned us about the danger of becoming whited sepulchers, respectable and apparently healthy on the outside, but suffering from the spiritual rigor mortis of *qesheh ʿoreph* on the inside. It's an image the prophets would have wholeheartedly endorsed. It's an image we American Christians need to take to heart so that we can begin the painful spiritual therapy of bending a stiffened neck. The recommended technique for doing so is falling to one's knees and clasping one's hands.

# Christian Mosaic

Let's play Jeopardy. The category is "Christianity," and the answer is "forty-three thousand."

If your response is "What's the number of Christian denominations worldwide?," congratulations.

The Center for the Study of Global Christianity estimates that the planet's two billion Christians embrace over forty thousand expressions of the faith. Roman Catholicism, Protestantism, and Orthodoxy lead the pack. But they've spawned thousands of sometimes quite unique offspring.

Under the Orthodox umbrella, there are, to name but a few, Russian Orthodox, Serbian Orthodox, Greek Orthodox, and Antiochian Orthodox self-governing jurisdictions. The number of autonomous non-Roman Catholic jurisdictions is steadily rising in both the United States and abroad. And the proliferation of independent Protestant denominations, especially in the southern hemisphere, is positively staggering.

That there are so many denominations is viewed by some Christians as a scandal. Christ wills, they believe, that his followers should all be united in a single sect, worship in a uniform way, and endorse the same theological doctrines. In support of their position, they cite a passage from John's Gospel in which Jesus prays that his followers may all "be one."

But Christians who lament what they see as the unholy fragmentation of the faith fail to grasp that unity isn't the same as uniformity. Consequently, they likewise fail, or perhaps refuse, to see that Christians the world over are already united when it comes to the essentials. Different denominations can and often do disagree about worship styles or theological priorities. But that's a sign of robustness, not fragmentation. It's good to keep in mind that the original apostles were themselves a motley bunch.

The sacrament of baptism makes all Christians, regardless of their denomination, members of one and the same body of Christ. It doesn't matter whether the baptism is performed by sprinkling a few drops of water on the head or submerging the entire body in a pool, nor whether it's given to infants or reserved for adults. Simply by virtue of their baptism, Christians are incorporated, as the Nicene Creed puts it, into the "one holy, catholic, and apostolic church," with "catholic" here designating "universal."

So all baptized believers, regardless of their traditions, belong to the body of Christ. The church is a multicolored mosaic, not a single-hued monolith.

Diversity, then, isn't a scandal. Genuine scandal arises when an overzealous denomination or jurisdiction fancies that it's got an absolute lock on the truth. Then irksome interdenominational quarrels erupt. Roman Catholics denounce independent Catholics as heretics, as if the Vatican somehow owns the word "Catholic," while charismatic Roman Catholics accuse their non-charismatic sisters and brothers of spiritual tepidity. Evangelicals denounce liberal Protestants for watering down the faith, and liberals fire back by saying that evangelicals read Scripture uncritically. Orthodox Christians deny the ultimate legitimacy of non-Orthodox Christianity, and sometimes even other Orthodox jurisdictions.

If anything can fragment Christianity, it's a stubborn refusal to acknowledge and celebrate the many ways in which fidelity to Christ can be expressed.

Saint Augustine said that anyone who claims to know God thereby proves that he or she actually doesn't. He realized, as have all great theologians, that no Christian can speak of God with anything approaching absolute authority. Even after the Incarnation, God remains the Great Mystery. Consequently, Christian denominations and jurisdictions would do well to adopt the humility appropriate to the essential unknowability of the God they worship. No single Christian sect can possibly have a monopoly on the truth; how could a sponge absorb the ocean? But the mosaic created by all forty-three thousand of them stretches our knowledge, dim as it is, of God.

This isn't a sloppy eclecticism that results in a patchwork God pieced together by thousands of seamstresses, but rather a broadening of perspective and an opening of mind and heart that encourages a rich ecumenism.

Roman Catholic priest Richard John Neuhaus, himself a former Lutheran, once wrote that when it comes right down to it, interdenominational squabbles over theology and doctrine properly give way to doxology. "Analysis and explanation," he noted, "finally dissolve into wonder and praise." Neuhaus is right. What ultimately unites all Christian sects is their shared baptismal fidelity to the God revealed in Christ. That's the unifying bottom line. When we stand before the Judgment Seat, God won't ask about which denominations we belonged to. There are no such things in heaven.

# Stripping Down

If there is an afterlife, and if it's permitted, I'd like to spend a few centuries chatting with Dietrich Bonhoeffer, the Lutheran pastor murdered by Nazi thugs in 1945.

Bonhoeffer, one of the most promising theologians of his generation, loathed everything about the Nazis. Hours after Hitler became Germany's chancellor in 1933, Bonhoeffer, then only in his mid-twenties, dared to mock him on the radio as the great Seducer (*Verfuhrer*) rather than the great Leader (*Fuhrer*). He also blasted the Nazi campaign against Jews and called on fellow Christians to resist it. It wasn't enough, he said, for the church to bandage victims crushed under Hitler's juggernaut. Christians were also called to jam up its wheels.

But many members of the German Lutheran Church that ordained Bonhoeffer disagreed. They happily hopped on the juggernaut and rode it to the very end. A disgusted Bonhoeffer helped found the oppositional Confessing Church, taught in its underground seminary, and collaborated in a plot against Hitler. The Gestapo finally arrested and imprisoned him in early 1943.

Although jailed, he didn't languish. Many readers, myself included, consider his writings from prison to be his best. During his two years behind bars, Bonhoeffer filled page after page with reflections on ethics, Scripture, society, faith, and the future of Christianity. It's his writing on this last topic that especially quickens the breath and sets the heart racing.

Most of us see the word "religion" as just a generic synonym for Christianity, Judaism, Islam, or any other faith tradition. Bonhoeffer thought so himself for most of his life. But during the long days and nights in prison, he moved toward the position that religion was actually a "garment" donned by Christianity, and that the theological and devotional cut of the suit changed from one historic period to the next.

The problem is that, somewhere along the line, Christians began mistaking the garment for Christianity itself. Bonhoeffer believed that this confusion sapped the vitality of the faith—evidenced, for example, by the enthusiasm with which many German Christians responded to Hitler.

Bonhoeffer argued that the garments worn for centuries by Christianity have exiled God from the world and cast him heavenwards as the Great Fixer, the All-Powerful Genie in the bottle, the Magic Wand we call upon only when we're in trouble. We want a God who rides in with the cavalry—religion's tepid substitution for Calvary—rescues us, and then conveniently rides off into the sunset. Christian religion, in short, exiles God to the margins of everyday, non-crisis life, to the "boundaries," as Bonhoeffer put it, "where human powers give out."

The solution? Christianity must strip itself of its religious garments and embrace its own nakedness.

Stripping Christianity of religion would invite the return of God from distant hinterlands and high altars back to "the middle of the village." God would cease being a churchy abstraction and become once more a welcome presence in the messy hustle and bustle of normal life. "Christ," wrote Bonhoeffer, would "no longer be an object of religion, but something quite different, really the Lord of the world"—with the emphasis here on "world." A Christianity purged of religion has no need of a Divine Handyman because it has rediscovered its core truth: God's real authority is expressed in powerlessness and humility, not majesty, might, and sorcery. For Bonhoeffer, "only the suffering God can help" us, not by magically fixing our problems, but by walking among us as one of us—and yet not simply as one of us, either—and by infusing meaning into our suffering by sharing it.

Stripped of its burdensome robes, a religionless Christianity becomes profoundly "this-worldly," in the same sense that Jesus was. Christians become daily companions of Jesus instead of people who gather together for an hour each week to mumble formulae to which they're often indifferent—except, of course, when they need something from Fixer God.

Bonhoeffer's prison reflections on religionless Christianity are often gnomic. The circumstances under which they were written prevented a more systematic treatment. But his goal throughout was to demonstrate that the Christianity he loved, when stripped of centuries of theological and cultural encrustations, was still relevant. Religious fashions come and go. Grace endures.

## Part 1: This Christian Thing

And for all this, the first thing I'd say to Bonhoeffer in paradise would be "thanks."

# Meeting the Enemy

I give up.

For years I've resisted the claim of my more conservative co-religionists that there's a war going on in this country against Christianity. But I'm throwing in the towel. Christianity is indeed under attack. The primary assailant, however, isn't secular elitism, shifting sexual norms, ethical relativism, or even (as disgraced pundit O'Reilly used to absurdly claim) hip-hop music. Instead, the war on Christianity is being waged by Christians. As the comic-strip character Pogo famously said, "We have met the enemy and he is us."

The Christian war against Christianity is conquering new territory every day. Recent casualty figures come from a "Religious Landscape Study" by the Pew Research Center. As of 2014, US adults willing to call themselves Christian hit an all-time low of 71 percent. Protestant and Roman Catholic congregations are hemorrhaging members in all regions of the nation, including the Bible Belt. Most of the people bailing are young adults—so-called millennials—college graduates, and affluent whites. The number of "nones," folks who neither profess or desire religious affiliation, is a staggering fifty-six million, or 23 percent of adults. 19 percent of them are ex-Christians. Atheists nearly doubled their numbers in the last decade. They now comprise 7 percent of American adults.[1]

By contrast, the numbers for non-Christian faiths in America are holding steady. This suggests that the downward trajectory of Christianity is more attributable to internal than external causes. People aren't abandoning the Jesus ship or refusing to board in the first place simply because they've been seduced by the golden calf of secularization. They're turning

---

1. Pew Research Center, "2014 Religious Landscape Study," https://www.pewforum.org/wp-content/uploads/sites/7/2015/05/RLS-II-FINAL-TOPLINE-FOR-FIRST-RELEASE.pdf, 159.

away because they're disgusted with priggish judgmentalism, bored out of their skulls by stuffy churchiness, or undernourished by misguided denominational efforts to be trendy.

Conservative Christians funnel too much of their energy into apocalyptic-toned moral condemnations of just about everything. An increasing number of Americans, especially young ones, have grown sick and tired of sledgehammer jeremiads against gay marriage, evolution, the ACLU, or any other obsession du jour conservative Protestants and Roman Catholics loudly serve up. Unfortunately, because the public too often uncritically assumes that conservative Christians accurately represent the faith, Christianity gets scornfully dismissed as a shill for the political right.

But it's not just conservative Christians who discredit Christianity. Moderate mainline and liberal denominations also contribute to the war effort.

Moderate mainline churches, frantic to stop the exodus of millennials, often rebrand worship as entertainment. Their assumption is that if they make Christianity hip and fun, they'll retain members and attract new ones. But pumped-up Christian rock bands and strobe syncopation in stadium-sized church buildings just don't work for two-thirds of all millennials. The Barna Group, a Christian think tank, discovered that the majority of young adults find such exhibitions slick, shallow, and inauthentic, leading them to associate Christianity with phony razzmatazz.

Liberal denominations assail Christianity by watering down or "demythologizing" doctrine so as not to offend anyone. This slash-and-burn strategy of clearing space for just about any belief reduces the resurrection of Jesus to metaphor, faith to a vague feel-goodism, and God to pretty much whatever one wants God to be. But the Barna Group reports that this anorexic approach actually repulses rather than attracts millennials. A full 67 percent of them find a scrubbed and bleached Christianity uncompelling.

There are, of course, thousands of American Christians who preach and practice the faith in ways that don't contribute to its corrosion. But the data show that they're losing ground to other Christians whose intolerant narrowness, glittery showmanship, or tepid wishy-washiness is driving millions away from the faith. It's quite true that the United States is an increasingly secular society. But the shift isn't the cause of Christianity's failure. It's the effect.

The perennial challenge for Christians is finding an idiom that effectively communicates the faith to each new generation. This requires carefully distinguishing between what's essential and what's merely peripheral, what's basic to the faith and what's best left to personal conscience. It's a task that requires humility, patience and prayer, each of which is poisoned when Christianity gets tied to political partisanship or rebranding gimmickry, or when it loses the fire in its belly. If liberal and conservative Christians alike don't wise up, the war we're unwittingly waging against the faith just might get won. We'll be victors whose triumph is our defeat.

# God-Wired

There's a scene in *The Power and the Glory*, Graham Greene's best novel, in which a boy chafes at having to listen to his mother read a treacly hagiography of a youthful saint named Juan. "Young Juan from his earliest years was noted for his humility and piety. We must not think that he did not laugh and play like other children, although there were times when he would creep away with a holy picture book."[1] Finally reaching his saturation point with this unedifying pablum, the boy, who's been ping-ponging between boredom and annoyance, shouts "I don't believe a word of it!" and storms out of the room.

I'm with him. I can't stomach those syrupy stories about saints who are always on their knees in histrionic prayer, hands clasped, eyes raised piously heavenward, too good, too pure, for this world. There's just something so inauthentically smarmy about those figures that I find myself wanting to smack rather than venerate them. They show up in biographies of the saints written for children as well as in some adult devotionals. But they're all humbug. Better a robust sinner than one of these sickeningly sweet caricatures.

For caricatures they are, products of a sentimentalism that prefers its religion served up as mawkish tripe. Genuine saints have the hard-edged feel of reality to them. They possess what poet T. S. Eliot called "wire in the blood," a spiritual electricity that positively hums with God-energy. Another poet, Gerard Manley Hopkins, wrote that God "crackles" in the world "like shook foil." So do God-wired saints.

There's a word for the God-voltage that lights them up: holiness. Holiness isn't a prim and proper piety. On the contrary, it's the risky resolve to love and serve God with everything one has. In the Christian tradition, this

---

1. Graham Greene, *The Power and the Glory* (New York: Penguin, 2003), 19.

means, as Saint Paul said, to "put on" Christ to such an extent that our will conforms to his. But of course all religions have saints, and it's a foolishly insular sectarianism that refuses to honor holy women and men from other traditions.

Holiness doesn't come in a one-size-fits-all uniform any more than it is the exclusive property of any one religion. Saints have different temperaments and talents, strengths and weaknesses, and the way they exhibit the God-wire in their blood inevitably reflects their individualities.

Some, like the soldier Saint Ignatius Loyola, are drawn to an active life; others, like the hermit Saint Anthony, to a more contemplative one. The faith of some saints is innocent as a child's, while other saints struggle with doubts and despair. Saint Teresa of Calcutta suffered mightily from the fear of death in her final days. A few saints were great sinners before they began to crackle with electric holiness; Saint Augustine falls into his category. But regardless of their individual styles or personal histories, what all saints have in common is risking all for God.

Just as we ought not to reduce saints to milquetoasts, neither should we promote them to demigods. Every single one of us, just like them, is God-wired. We too are commissioned to reflect God's love as brightly as sparks shooting from shook foil, and the saints we honor, individually on their feast days and collectively on All Saints' Day, remind us of this. Their examples inspire us to awaken to what the Trappist monk Thomas Merton said was the true calling of everyone: sainthood. Each and every one of us is born to be a saint. A saint is simply—and marvelously—a human fully alive.

Growing into sainthood isn't an easy task for many of us, immersed as we are in a culture that encourages us to focus on ego gratification at the expense of heeding the vibration of the wire in our blood. Perhaps that's why we so often transform saints into insipid fictions who conveniently make no real demands on us. It may also account for why so many of us prefer a God who's just as toothlessly accommodating.

Emulating real saints instead of marzipan ones like Juan can be an electrifying experience, and the jolt sometimes smarts. But it also galvanizes the God-wire in our blood, charging up our own yearning for holiness. And once that happens, we're well on our way to becoming shook foil that crackles with God.

# Slaves and Masters

A religion for slaves, weaklings, and fools: that's what the nineteenth-century philosopher Friedrich Nietzsche, who liked to call himself the antichrist, thought of Christianity.

Nietzsche, the son of a Lutheran pastor, argued that early Christians, whom he incorrectly assumed were mostly slaves, were too pathetically weak to embrace the noble virtues—battlefield valor, pride, physical strength, and self-sufficient autonomy—he attributed to their masters.

So, he argued, the first followers of Jesus adopted an alternative set of ignoble norms—humility, meekness, self-sacrifice, loving-kindness, nonviolence, and so on—more compatible with their slavish spinelessness, and then defended their craven code of conduct by insisting that Jesus practiced it and commanded his followers to do likewise. As Christianity spread, its perverse morality infected the four corners of the world.

This transition from master to slave morality, thundered Nietzsche, was the greatest crime perpetrated against humanity. It emasculated our wills and drowned us in mewling timidity.

Nietzsche was neither the first nor the last skeptic to argue that Christianity is a religion tailor-made for weaklings. Several philosophers in the eighteenth-century Enlightenment said as much; in the early twentieth century, Freud famously argued that Christians who fearfully cling to God suffered from arrested emotional development; and in our own day, the loud but not terribly coherent atheists Richard Dawkins and Sam Harris beat the same drum.

There's no denying that some Christians, just like people of other or no faith traditions, are temperamentally anxious, skittish, or conflict-aversive. But to claim that the early Christians made a virtue out of necessity by masquerading their slavish timidity as spiritual strength simply doesn't accord with historical fact.

Consider, for example, the original disciples of Jesus. Far from being trembling wallflowers, they were roughly-hewn men and women of the world who knew how to take care of themselves. Many of the original twelve apostles were fisherman who worked long hours casting their nets, braving sudden storms on the Sea of Galilee, struggling to make ends meet, and welcoming a couple of pints and some lively carousing with their mates after the day's catch was sold.

One of the Twelve, Simon, was a zealot, a pugnacious resister of the Roman occupation. The apostle Matthew, a tax collector before joining Jesus, must've had pretty thick skin to withstand the scorn of fellow Jews who saw him as a Roman collaborator. And even though the apostles temporarily panicked at Jesus's arrest, all of them, with the sole exception of John, went on to die for their faith, as have countless other Christians up to the present day. History is bespattered with the gore of martyred Christians.

Nietzsche's claim that the early Christians were milquetoasts is countered by a word that appears forty times in the New Testament to describe Jesus's followers: *parrhesia*. It means "bold speech" or "straightforward speech that conceals nothing" in intimidating or threatening circumstances. *Parrhesia* connotes joyful confidence, boldness, and fearlessness, especially when it comes to defying misused authority. This is hardly the behavior one expects from cowardly slaves who pump up their own weaknesses into virtues.

What critics fail to recognize is that the Christian values they reject as feeble or cowardly in fact demand great courage and self-discipline. Humility and meekness, far from being characteristics of weaklings, are cultivated by persons who refuse to succumb to the temptation of egoism. Sacrifice for the sake of others is a mark of love and devotion, not of pathetic surrender. In a world that resorts to recrimination and bloodshed at the drop of a hat, nonviolent resistance to evil calls for incredible bravery and steadfastness. In a culture that encourages bluster, boasting, shrieking, and drowning out the voices of others, the practice of *parrhesia* calls for vigilant self-discipline.

This isn't a slave religion. On the contrary, it's the "master values" defended by Nietzsche that bind us with shackles of arrogance, egoism, and self-indulgence. The narcissist, the powermonger, the sybarite, the lone wolf who claims not to need anyone: these, not Christians, are the people truly enslaved by weakness.

As the author of Galatians wrote, Christ freed his followers from the yoke of bondage by offering an alternative to master values.

This is something the Nietzsches of the world just don't get.

# Wedding Joy

There's a church sign that makes me cringe every time I drive past it. It invites all and sundry to "Come and Hear the Word of God!"

Now, in itself this isn't a bad message. The sign's cringe-worthiness is the biblical quotation that follows, which the sponsoring church apparently believes best summarizes what God wants everyone to hear: "The wages of sin is death!"

From a purely marketing perspective, this sour note isn't likely to attract many people to Christianity. It's as if a tobacco manufacturer erected a billboard announcing: "The good news about cigarettes is that they give you heart disease and cancer!"

From the more important vantage point of faith, the church sign desperately distorts the Good News, turning it into a gloomy breast-beating and finger-pointing mockery of Christ's message. In fact, the quotation about sin isn't even from Jesus. It's an out-of-context snippet from Paul's letter to the Romans.

No disrespect to Paul, but surely the go-to guy when it comes to the word of God ought to be Jesus, *the* Word, not one of his followers.

There are two interpretations of Christianity which have danced with one another over the centuries. Sometimes one is in the ascendancy, sometimes the other. For the last few years, at least in the United States, the second has been top dog.

The first interpretation has it that the world is fundamentally a good place, a gift from God to be celebrated, enjoyed, and cared for; that humans, despite our lapses into stupidity and wickedness, are basically good too, made as we are in the likeness of God; that God created a rational universe and endowed us with reason, the use of which is pleasing to God; and that the word best associated with God is "love."

The second believes that the world is fundamentally fallen, a bleak place of constant temptation that seeks to mire us ever deeper in wickedness; that we're easy marks for corruption, broken as we are by original sin; that the ways of God are inscrutable; that reason is suspect and properly subservient to faith; and that the word best associated with God is "judgment."

I suspect that these two perspectives have a lot to do with temperament. Some people just naturally seem to be inclined to gloom and others to joy. But temperament aside, insisting that the bottom-line word of God is about sin and human depravity is simply false. This bleak and recriminatory message is responsible for generations of Christians needlessly suffering from self-loathing—what was once called "scrupulousness," a neurotic focusing on one's faults—and generations of joylessly blue-nosed clergy specializing in fire-and-brimstone jeremiads.

For wages-of-sin-is-death Christians, faith is a hammer, and the simplest, most innocent pleasures of life are all nails. Such heralds of bad news seem to forget that the first miracle Christ performed was turning water into wine at the wedding feast in Cana, a celebration of love in which laughter, music, song, dance, and wine were plentiful.

Later, when Jesus publicly revealed who he was, did he thunderously proclaim that humans are sinners in the hands of an angry God? No. He came, he said, to preach good news to the poor, to proclaim release to the captives, to give vision to the blind, liberation to the oppressed, and forgiveness to all.

Little wonder that good Pope John XXIII, canonized in 2014, felt obliged to publicly disagree with "those prophets of gloom, who are always forecasting disaster, as though the end of the world were at hand." The word of God is about hope, love, and joy. The joy isn't a naïve feel-goodism, but the grateful awareness that the universe is saturated with God's saving love.

Were I to invite people to hear the word of God, what scriptural passage would I pick? "As the Father loves me, so I love you" comes to mind. So does "My yoke is easy and my burden light" and "Love God with all your heart, soul, mind, and strength, and your neighbor as yourself." And let's not forget, "Do not judge, lest you be judged."

Or perhaps it would be best simply to invite them to the wedding, and remind them to bring their dancing shoes.

# PART 2

# The Spiritual Life

# Loneliness

Fifteen years ago, I nearly drowned.

At that time, my family and I lived in the Caribbean nation of Barbados. On the day of my misadventure, we were picnicking on one of the island's beaches. I hopped in the surf and splashed further away from shore than I should've, because I'm not a good swimmer. To be honest, I can't really swim at all. I just sort of wade.

Suddenly the ocean floor dropped out from under me and I sank like the proverbial stone. Instantly aware that I was in serious trouble, I panicked, struggling again and again to push myself up above the water. Each time I managed to break the surface for a mouthful of air, I caught glimpses of my wife and son on the beach, completely unaware of my plight. I was so close to them—no more than a couple hundred yards—and yet also so far, far away.

I've never felt more absolutely alone.

After what seemed like forever, I finally felt the ocean floor once more under my feet, and staggered my way back to shore.

I'll always remember my near-drowning with a shudder. But over the years, I've come to realize that it was my sense of utter loneliness, and not the fear of actually dying, which made the experience so terrible. In fact, it's precisely because dying is something we must do completely on our own that it's so fearsome.

Even if we're surrounded by loved ones as we lie on our deathbeds, we still make the final journey without companions to comfort and strengthen us. It's understandable that the prospect of such radical loneliness frightens us; we dread the absence of companionship even on this side of the grave.

Loneliness oughtn't to be confused with solitude. We all need regular periods by ourselves to step away from the rat race, examine our priorities, and think about who we are. Solitude helps us expand. Loneliness, on the other hand, contracts minds and hearts, making us feel so abandoned that our spirits hunker down in despair. In loneliness, we experience a disorienting slippage of self, a state of forlorn invisibility atremble with the fear that we're unnoticed by others and utterly on our own.

The lonely person knows what it's like to feel the waters of the deep closing over her head, and to have people only a few feet away completely oblivious of her.

Joseph Ratzinger, a very insightful theologian who's unfortunately more vilified than actually read, points out that "the abyss of loneliness" always threatens humans. Even the God-man Jesus experienced its constriction at least twice: on the night of his capture, when he wrestled in Gethsemane with the loneliness of impending death while his boon companions slept, and during his final moments on the cross when he shrieked in despair at God's abandonment of him.

What's the antidote to the loneliness that breeds such anguish? Dorothy Day, cofounder of the Catholic Workers movement, said it well: "We have all known the long loneliness and we have learned that the only solution is love, and that comes with community." By "community" she means communion, not the handful of casual acquaintances or Facebook friends that often passes for community these days. Genuine community has a vertical as well as a horizontal dimension. When we open ourselves in love and service to our fellow humans, we become part of a fellowship that chisels away at our loneliness. But human companionship, if it's to be truly fulfilling, must be buttressed by a loving relationship with the God who anchors communion.

Only in the crossed beams of horizontal and vertical love do we find the community that can offer us some relief from the lonesome invisibility that kindles fear.

At the same time, however, let's not deceive ourselves. Ratzinger is right: as long as we're alive, we're susceptible to loneliness. And there's no getting around the fact that each of us will die alone. But the Christian believes that the Resurrected Christ defeated death. This of course doesn't mean that we won't physically die, or that our passing will be any less unaccompanied. But it does mean that the loneliness of death doesn't have the last word, and that no matter how alone and helpless we feel, we'll make it to shore.

# Zombies

We just can't seem to get enough of zombies. They're everywhere: comics, novels, television shows, movies, scholarly conferences, college courses, and even PhD dissertations. Type "zombies" into a Google search and you'll get over 340 million hits.

So we're clearly fascinated. But why? How is it that the "living dead," animated corpses with a savage hunger for human flesh, have so captured our imaginations? Here's the short answer: they satisfy a powerful archetypal need that most of us aren't even consciously aware of having.

More than a century ago, sociologist Max Weber argued that as societies grow increasingly secular, their corporate understanding of reality transitions from "enchanted" to "disenchanted."

For our ancestors, says Weber, reality was "enchanted," shimmering with "mysterious incalculable forces," typically expressed in religious language, which superimposed transcendent meaning on everyday life. But for secularized moderns, all this is implausible. Reason has replaced faith, and science has demolished the religious beliefs by which our ancestors oriented themselves. We dwell in a "disenchanted" or "desacralized" world.

Well, not quite. The truth of the matter is that no society ever becomes fully secularized. The hunger for a transcendent dimension to reality—for an enchanted world—remains a basic human drive, and if it can't express itself in overtly religious imagery, it'll search out symbolic substitutes. So, for example, psychologists become modernity's priests, invested with awesome authority to hear confessions, bless, and heal. Political allegiances substitute for religious communities, and partisan feuds take on the rhetoric of cosmic struggles. Self-improvement replaces spiritual discernment. Patriotic holidays and rituals stand in for religious holy days. Our chthonic yearning for something greater than ourselves plays out again and again, even in a supposedly disenchanted world.

## Part 2: The Spiritual Life

One important archetype that gets renamed and redistributed in modern society is metaphysical evil, or the devil. Its psychological importance can't be underestimated; it helps us cope with those acts of wickedness—torture, genocide, child abuse—so numbingly sinister that chalking them up to mere human agency is unsatisfyingly inadequate. Our ancestors personified metaphysical evil in the form of a demonic enemy, Satan, who roams the world like a roaring lion seeking human prey. Their "enchanted" belief in the devil's machinations provided them with an explanation for evil that protected them from the far worse alternative that wickedness is meaninglessly gratuitous and spontaneous. Moreover, it gave purposeful direction to their lives by offering them the opportunity to enlist in God's grim but ultimately triumphant crusade against evil.

Most people today, even religious ones, no longer believe in the reality of a metaphysical source of evil, much less its personification as Satan. (Dinosaur that I am, however, I do.) Nor have they an explicit sense of soldiering in a cosmic battle between divine good and hellish evil. But both archetypes are so hardwired in our psyches that they recur again and again, finding a home in any symbol that can express them.

And here's where we cue the zombies. They're today's devils, modernity's version of the Great Enemy. We re-enchant the world by attributing to zombies qualities that our ancestors believed belonged to Satan. Zombies allow us to scratch our itch for archetypal symbols that hold deep meaning for us while allowing us to jettison pre-modern religious language that no longer speaks to us.

So for us, zombies become roaring satanic lions hungrily searching out prey. They're concrete personifications of our deep and ancient sense that evil is somehow mysteriously nonhuman in origin even though it uses humans as its agents. Zombies reek of death and the grave—the underground, where Satan and the damned traditionally dwell. Their bite mutates human victims into zombies, just as Satan's embrace mutates humans into slaves. And the cosmic battle theme between good and evil is also present: in all zombie stories, a valiant band of humans, typically led by a Savior-like figure, risk their own lives to rescue humankind from damnation.

Hardly anyone believes that zombies actually exist. But our fascination with them points to the latest recurrence of the very same archetype which for earlier generations was communicated in explicitly religious language. We are more deeply rooted in the enchanted world of our ancestors than we suspect.

So the next time you watch a zombie movie, be aware that your forebears are seated alongside you.

# Original Blessing

Jonathan Edwards's 1741 "Sinners in the Hands of an Angry God" is arguably the most famous sermon ever preached on American soil. It's also one of the most ferocious jeremiads to come out of the eighteenth-century Protestant revival known as the First Great Awakening.

The fire-and-brimstone sermon is vintage Edwards. A loyal Calvinist, he never faltered in his adherence to the doctrine of total depravity, which declares that since the fall, we humans are so firmly mired in wickedness that our intellects and wills are utterly corrupt. No human escapes the taint of original sin, passed down from our wayward ancestors Adam and Eve.

Because of our inherent wickedness, our only hope of salvation is the gratuitous mercy of God, who predestines some of us for heaven but most of us for hell—another rather dismal Calvinist doctrine. Those of us bound for perdition, Edwards thundered, are suspended over hellfire by fragile threads that can snap at any moment.

I've reread this particular sermon with some regularity over the last four decades, not because I agree with Edwards, but because I see his sermon as a salutary reminder of what happens when Christianity goes bad.

The authentic message of Christianity is one of joyful liberation. It's undeniable that we humans are prone to sin. Anyone with even the slightest self-insight knows this to be true.

But what Edwards and his like-minded successors forget is that humans are made in the likeness of God, a likeness whose details are sharpened by the life, teachings, and resurrection of Jesus.

To be made in the likeness of an all-loving and all-good God means that we're inherently good and godly creatures, not helplessly wicked. Our God-given capacity for virtue is prior to and more powerful than our attraction to sin. So instead of fixating, as Edwards does, on the recriminatory doctrine of original sin, we should shift our focus to what theologian

Matthew Fox calls our "Original Blessing": the wondrous fact that God loves us into existence and sustains us, moment by moment, with a ceaselessly generous outpouring of grace.

Rejecting Edwards's harsh interpretation of Christianity is neither a soft-pedaling of sin nor a denial of the importance of shame and repentance when we commit evil. But it does mean that we cease thinking of God as a terrifyingly fierce hanging judge more eager to condemn than to love.

I suspect that if we chronicled all the damage done by the pushers of original sin and angry God—and they stretch at least as far back as the fifth-century Saint Augustine—we'd be shocked. Abused children frequently grow into abusive adults. Bombard generations of children with the self-hating lesson that original sin makes them forever unworthy of God's love and chances are good that they'll become adults crippled by a pathological sense of guilt and a joylessly stiff-necked judgmentalism that sees sinfulness everywhere.

Everything that Jesus taught about God runs contrary to Edwards's angry God. Jesus never turned a blind eye to sin. He neither practiced nor recommended a bland I'm-ok-you're-ok spirituality. Instead, whenever he encountered the soul sickness of sin, he rebuked the prodigal and then offered healing and forgiveness, seven times seventy if necessary. He did so because he saw God's likeness shining through all persons, no matter how deeply they were sunk in sin. He wanted to let them know that God's hands are lovingly open, not angrily clenched.

That Christians like Augustine and Edwards have perversely morphed Jesus's message of love, compassion, and generosity into an obsession with sin is a genuine tragedy that continues, even now, to drown out the good news with very bad news indeed. The predictable consequence is that people genuinely hungry for God are dismayed when told that they're unworthy of him. They need, and they deserve, to be reassured that God lovingly yearns for them, just as much as they long for God.

Edwards's image in "Sinners" of an angry deity dangling us over hell is as cruel as it is misleading. But thankfully the sermon can serve as a cautionary tale. Although he didn't intend it, Edwards's bleak message invites us to reflect on the truths that love, not fear, is how God calls us to relate to God, and that original blessing trumps original sin. God's hands are always ready to catch us when we fall.

# Gorged But Starving

Remember Gordon Gekko, the cutthroat corporate raider in Oliver Stone's 1987 film *Wall Street* whose appetite for money, power, and sex was as unquenchable as it was destructive?

In what became the movie's signature scene, Gekko triumphantly proclaimed, "Greed is good!"

That three-word phrase could be the mantra of today's consumerist culture. The rest of us may not have the moxie to be as upfront as Gekko about the insatiability of our appetites. But let's face it. Too many of us have been bitten by the Gekko bug. We want to gorge on everything—luxuries, thrills, influence, wealth, fame—and we want to do it now.

Every year, Muslims around the world remind us that there's another way to live. They observe Ramadan, their tradition's annual thirty-day period of fasting. One of the "Five Pillars" of Islam—the others are affirming God and Muhammad, prayer, almsgiving, and pilgrimage—Ramadan obliges participants to abstain from food, drink, and tobacco during daylight hours.

To a society addicted to instant gratification, fasting for any reason other than physical health or appearance comes across as senseless and even masochistic. Why deprive oneself? Life's too short! Even many Jews and Christians have a hard time with the idea of fasting. For them, it's a largely meaningless practice that they halfheartedly, if at all, observe. They may have a vague sense that it's good to fast on Yom Kippur or to give something up for Lent, but aren't quite sure why.

Yet the primary purpose of fasting isn't simply to give something up. Abstention is the means, not the end. We fast to jolt ourselves into a moment of clarity. Fasting is a spiritual discipline intended to break our Gekko compulsion to gorge on junk food long enough for us to discern what our hearts really desire and what's really good for us. In the Christian tradition, the iconic story about facing down the temptation to gorge on immediate gratification, glory, and power is Jesus's fast in the wilderness. It gave him the wisdom needed for his public ministry. It showed him what was important and what wasn't.

We lose sight of what's genuinely important and hence desirable because our compulsion to gorge—a word derived, appropriately, from the Latin for "whirlpool" or "maelstrom"—is a furious turbulence that swirls us round and round in a spiral of frustrated craving. To appease our terrible hunger pangs, we indiscriminately cram everything we can lay hands on down our gullets. But because what we're eating isn't what we truly need to satisfy our hunger, the more we gorge, the more we starve.

Our deepest hunger, which in our confusion we try to satisfy with Gekko junk food, is for what spiritual teachers across the centuries have called truth, beauty, and goodness. Each of us has an innate yearning, a fundamental soul-hunger, for contact with these three profoundly satisfying values because we know at our deepest level that they hold the secret of genuine fulfillment. We crave the serenity of truth, the eternity of beauty, and the purity of goodness. It's just that too often we settle for pale substitutes: chit-chat and gossip, passing fashion and fad, and cynical relativism.

Even the most frenzied gorgers catch occasional glimpses of what their hearts truly desire. There isn't a person alive who at some time or another hasn't been electrified by an "Aha!" experience of truth, awed by a beauty-saturated poem or sunset, or humbled before a genuinely selfless act of goodness. Fasting calms the furious waters of gorging to allow these peripheral experiences to move to centerstage. Once that happens, Gekko junk food loses its seductive allure. Our priorities change.

For people of faith, the clarity of vision that fasting can bring inevitably points to the divine Source who transcends the physical world, yet infuses meaning into it. The soul's yearning for truth, beauty, and goodness, at its more profound level, is always a longing for God, even if we don't recognize it as such. "Like the deer panting for cool streams of water," sings the Psalmist, "so my heart pants for Thee, O Lord" (Ps 42:1). Muslims who devoutly fast during Ramadan know this. In their tradition, God has no fewer than ninety-nine distinct names. And three of them are truth, beauty, and goodness.

# Kissing God

If God seems a distant abstraction to you, you might want to take a look at a book in the Bible that you've likely never heard preached from the pulpit, and most definitely never learned about in Sunday school. Its opening line gives a sizzling indication of the entire book's temperature: "Oh, that you would kiss me with the kisses of your mouth, for your love is sweeter than wine!"

I'm talking about the Song of Songs, one of the Wisdom books in the Hebrew Scriptures. It's sandwiched between the doleful Ecclesiastes and the long and beautiful text attributed to the prophet Isaiah. Everybody's familiar with at least a couple of lines from Ecclesiastes ("To everything there is a season" or "Vanity of vanities, all is vanity"), and Christians hear Isaiah's description (via Handel, if in no other way) of the suffering servant ("a man lowly and despised") every Christmas. But the Song of Songs goes largely unnoticed. Too bad.

We've no idea who wrote the Song (even though tradition gives King Solomon credit) nor when it was written (although 400 BC is a pretty good guess). What we do know is that it's one of ancient literature's sexiest tributes to erotic love. In a dialogue that's sometimes coy and sometimes brazen, a lover and her beloved express their yearning for one another. "Your breasts are two fawns, twins of a gazelle, grazing in a field of lilies," the beloved whispers. "I am in the fever of love!" the lover responds. "Come, let us lie all night among the flowering henna."

For centuries, the poem's heady erotic passion was allegorized away by commentators who apparently thought it too hot and heavy for a sacred book. Jews read the lover and her beloved as stand-ins for Israel and Yahweh, Christians for the church and Christ. The couple's mutual yearning was seen as a symbol of the soul's desire for God and God's desire to be loved.

Now, I'm totally in agreement with reading the Song as a celebration of the relationship between God and humans. But we ought to avoid a prudish temptation to overly spiritualize the undeniably erotic language used to express that relationship. The Song's unknown author deliberately likened our yearning for God to the erotic desire of lovers. He or she must have had a reason.

Think of it like this. Eros is an intensely passionate yearning for the beloved. Far from being the groin-centered titillation we confuse it with, eros engages the entire person, body and mind. When we love erotically, we positively ache to be joined with the beloved, to submerge our identity into his or hers, to become so intimately fused with him or her that the boundaries between self and the other dissolve, even if only for a few seconds. It's why the French insightfully (and delicately) call sexual climax *le petite mort*, or "the little death."

The act of erotic love melds human lovers, and the author of the Song obviously believes that the language of lovemaking is an appropriate metaphorical expression of our heart-longing for union with the divine Beloved. Our pining for the kisses of God's mouth is (or at least should be) so intense that only *le grand mort*, the "great death" of dissolving into the Beloved, will satisfy.

In this kind of longing, the conventional distinction between body and spirit disappears. Our whole person, our entire being, is consumed by God-desire, and God, who never holds anything back, ardently rushes to embrace us. The Song's author expresses the consummation with moving tenderness: "My Beloved is mine and I am his." Saint Paul describes the consummation of his own yearning more vividly: "it is not I who live, but Christ who lives in me."

It's not surprising that so many Hindu, Jewish, Christian, and Muslim mystics draw upon the language of erotic love to describe their union with the divine Beloved. In the Christian tradition, the sixteenth-century Saint Teresa of Avila's description is probably the most famous, and the most explicit. She describes an angel piercing her with an upward-driven "golden shaft" that causes her to swoon from "the sweetness of excessive pain." Teresa lay with her Beloved among the flowering henna, and knew what it was to love and be loved by God.

Body-despising prudes might find Teresa's words shocking. But the Song's author wouldn't. Neither should we.

# God's Need for Love

Readers of a certain age will remember the "Baltimore Catechism," a formidably uninspiring question-and-answer summary of the faith endured by three generations of American Roman Catholics.

Early on, the Catechism asks "Why did God make you?" and tersely responds: "God made me to know Him, to love Him, and to serve Him in this world."

This response is an okay start, but it strikes me as a little lopsided. I think it could use supplementing with an insight expressed centuries ago in the *Brihadaranyaka Upanishad*, one of the Hindu sacred texts: God, or Brahman, created humans because he was lonely, and loneliness slays joy and delight.

God created us not simply that we might love and serve him, but that he might love us and derive joy from our companionship. In other words, it's not just that we humans need God; God needs us, too.

God needs to love and be loved.

This observation goes against the grain of a school of Christian theology that insists on the "impassability" of God. "Impassable" simply means "unable to experience or undergo emotions." It's an utterly unbiblical understanding of God, but thanks to the influence of the Greek philosopher Aristotle, it's been around for centuries.

Aristotle argued that God is an "unmoved mover," an utterly self-contained being impervious to outside influence. His reasoning was that God is perfect by definition, and something that is perfect is incapable of being changed. Change either enriches or diminishes that which is changed. But perfection can neither be enriched (how can something perfect be made more perfect?), nor diminished (how then could it have been perfect in the first place?).

Now, the ability to love, to feel the bite of loneliness, or to crave companionship implies changeability. When we love someone, we're moved by their joy as well as their pain. When we're lonely, we acknowledge a gap in our lives that cries out to be filled. When we yearn for companionship, we confess that we're not self-sufficient, but in need of others.

None of this, argued Aristotle, is worthy of God. God must be perfect, and hence impassable. God doesn't need anything, much less petty little humans.

Aristotelian-inspired theologians have tried to reconcile the impassably perfect Unmoved Mover with the biblical God by arguing that the latter actually does love, but in an abstractly emotionless (changeless) way. Others have insisted that the three Persons of the Trinity ceaselessly love one another, but in a self-enclosed unchanging manner.

Yet neither of these maneuvers is convincing. Abstract love is unworthy of the name, and the sealed-off love of the Trinitarian God is suspiciously like a revamping of Aristotle's self-contained Unmoved Mover.

Thankfully, in recent years, Christian theologians have begun to take seriously what most everyday Christians have always known: that the biblical portrait of God affirms him as rejoicing and suffering with us, and ceaselessly desiring—needing—to love and be loved by us.

These same theologians are starting to recognize that perfection doesn't require unchangeability, and that embracing vulnerability for the sake of love is a strength rather than a weakness in both humans and God. They're beginning to appreciate that the God who covenants with us and incarnates to become one of us shares our deepest joys and most painful wounds, both of which allow him to enter ever more deeply into empathic relationship with us.

This God so loves us and so needs us to love him in return that he disdains to play it safe by hiding behind divine impassability. He willingly forgoes it for the sake of a genuinely living rather than merely formal communion with humanity.

Realizing that God needs our love, as well as knowing from firsthand experience that we flourish when we're loved and suffer when we're not, can profoundly affect how we relate to God. That God needs us just as we need him underscores the awesome importance of offering him our love. The human-divine relationship ceases to be a lopsided one in which all the giving is God's and all the taking is ours, and instead becomes one of mutual dependence—as any genuinely loving relationship is.

## Part 2: The Spiritual Life

Loneliness, the *Brihadaranyaka Upanishad* affirms, is a dismal slayer of happiness. So let us be God's boon companions. Let us offer him joy.

# Becoming Prayer

In the third and fourth centuries, scores of Christians fled villages, towns, and cities for the barren outbacks of Egypt and Syria. These so-called desert fathers and mothers searched for God, as had Abraham, John the Baptist, and Jesus before them, in the silence and solitude of the wilderness. They strove through prayer and fasting to strip away whatever stood between them and their Creator.

Many stories about them have come down to us. Here's one of them.

A young and frustrated novice goes to Abba Joseph, a desert hermit especially noted for holiness. "Master," the youth says, "I diligently fast, meditate, and read the Scriptures. Yet I seem to get nowhere spiritually. Tell me, I beg you. What more must I do?"

Abba Joseph rises to his feet, looks heavenward, holds up his hands, and his outstretched fingers suddenly look like ten blazing torches. "If you truly want it," the old man says to the astounded novice, "you can become flame."

We aren't told if the novice persevered until he, too, eventually burst into flame. But the advice he got is as valuable today as it was all those centuries ago.

What Abba Joseph shared was the secret of deep prayer.

When we think of prayer, most of us have in mind either formulaic ones, like the Christian "Our Father" or the Jewish *Sh'ma* (the Shema), or extemporaneous ones that, depending on the context, express gratitude, contrition, or need. There's absolutely nothing wrong with such prayers. They're perfectly legitimate ways of reaching out to God.

But the desert hermits wanted to go deeper. For them, memorized and extemporaneous prayers were embers that warmed the soul but lacked the intensity to ignite a transformative blaze.

## Part 2: The Spiritual Life

They discovered that the secret to the more profound prayer experience they desired was to cultivate an utterly uninhibited flowing toward God, an attentiveness so concentrated and focused that all traces of self are left behind and replaced with a nakedly unselfconscious awareness of the Divine.

When an individual reaches this point, the desert fathers and mothers discovered, she's no longer "doing" prayer, but has become prayer itself. She's been transformed from pray-er to prayer.

Or, as Abba Joseph demonstrated with his fingers, the ember blazes forth as flame.

If this sounds strange to you, consider analogues from everyday life. You and I can become so engrossed in a novel or a film that our self-awareness of reading or watching disappears. Our habitual way of dividing the world into subject and object vanishes, and we enter so deeply into the novel or film that we become participants, not onlookers.

Long-distance runners are familiar with the experience of entering the "flow zone," that state of focused awareness in which they lose a sense of distinction between themselves and what they're doing. They're no longer simply runners. Now, at least while the flow lasts, they're the running itself.

Finally, consider common experiences in which our attention is riveted on a particular event or idea. We transcend our entrenched self-awareness to focus so intensely and exclusively on what's fascinated us that once again the subject/object dichotomy collapses for a few moments. We become sheer attentiveness.

Striving for such uninhibited focus was the reason desert mothers and fathers fled to the wilderness. Their goal was to liberate themselves from the minutiae of busy lives that too often block prayerful flow to God.

But getting rid of distractions, while necessary for transformative prayer, isn't sufficient. When we pray, we're not engrossed by a novel, aiming for a runner's high, or fascinated by a news item. Prayer, as Abba Joseph said, begins as an act of the will: "if you truly want it," he told the novice.

"Wanting it" means willing as intimate a relationship with God as is possible this side of the grave. This kind of willing is sustained only by love so strong that it's egoless and unconditional enough to be exclusively directed toward the divine Source that graciously overflows itself to create and sustain everything that is.

Loving God in this way, with all one's heart, soul, mind, and strength, as both Hebrew and Christian Scriptures recommend, is what combusts ember into flame.

And when this happens, the pray-er becomes prayer.

# Divine *Nada*

Ernest Hemingway's story "A Clean, Well-Lighted Place" is haunting, although not necessarily in the way he intended. Hemingway meant it to evoke a sense of alienated despair. But it can also be read as an inadvertent homage to what Saint John of the Cross, the great sixteenth-century Christian mystic, tells us about God.

Hemingway's story centers on two old men in an all-night café who are burdened by a relentless sense of meaninglessness. When the dark nights come and their despair deepens, they seek out temporary havens in "clean and well-lighted" public bars and bistros. But the clinking of glasses and the laughter of patrons offer no real relief from their despondent conviction that there is neither God, intrinsic meaning to life, or possibility of redemption. In an absurd universe, such beliefs are illusions.

Their weary melancholy, Hemingway believes, is the characteristic signature of a modern age that has lost faith. As one of the old men mutters, "Our *nada* who art in *nada*, *nada* be thy name, thy kingdom *nada* thy will be *nada* in *nada* as it is in *nada*. Give us this *nada* our daily *nada* and *nada* us our *nada* as we *nada* our *nadas* and *nada* us not into *nada*, but deliver us from *nada*. Hail nothing full of nothing, nothing is with thee."

*Nada*, nothing: that's the dreadful vacuum to which Hemingway believes we're condemned, and he sees no way out. We're orphaned the moment we're born, abandoned in a universe both empty and silent. We live futile lives, and then we die. Period.

Most of us probably have had moments in which the universe seemed hideously cold and indifferent. Like Hemingway's old men, we've glimpsed emptiness and shuddered. But John of the Cross looked into the same inky depths and discovered a Presence there that nourished rather than crushed his spirit. He sensed God, and in joyful exultation rather than hopeless despair cried out, "*Nada, nada, nada, nada, nada, nada, nada!*" The God he discovered was, he wrote, "*todo y nada*," all and nothing, and God's voice was "*la musica callada*," silent music.

This is bewildering. How can something be both all and nothing? How can music be silent? How can silence be heard?

Saint John was an apophatic (from the Greek verb "to negate or deny") mystic who believed that divine mystery is so impenetrable that the best we can do when speaking about God is to state, *ad seriatim*, what God is not. God is neither this nor that; God is not like anything in the physical world, even though we too frequently slip into the habit of talking about God in the same way we talk about objects. God is literally No-thing, inexhaustibly transcending all finite beings. Yet at the same time, God is All, the necessary Source and Ground of everything that exists. *Todo y nada.*

The Holy Spirit simply doesn't have words to communicate the incomprehensible reality of God, nor have humans the intellects to understand even if there were words. So to our ears, God's voice is silent. But if we learn how to listen, we discover, as John did, that it's a silence pregnant with meaning, and that it speaks to the deepest and purist part of us.

Remember the Hebrew Bible's story of Elijah's encounter with the silent music of God? Elijah awaits God, fully expecting a flashy, Academy-Award-winning theophany. But to his amazement, he discovers that God isn't to be heard in furious winds, heaving earthquakes, or scorching fires, but rather in a "still, small voice."

Both Elijah and John learned that our best chance of contact with the divine Nada is disciplining ourselves simply to listen, in patient repose, for the still voice, God's silent music, and to allow ourselves to sink into its depths.

The experiences of mystics from all faith traditions testify that none of us can hope for a greater intimacy with God than this. Even Christ, who took on human form and pitched his tent in our midst, is ultimately unfathomable. As the evangelist John says, there aren't enough words in the world to explain the Incarnate Word.

That's why Hemingway's "our *nada* who art in *nada*" is closer to the truth than he imagined. We can neither comprehend nor adequately describe Divine Nada. But we can joyfully experience it and gratefully pray to it.

# We Are God's Wombs

Saint Teresa of Avila (1515–82) is often credited with saying that we humans are the eyes, hands, and feet of God. "Christ," she wrote, "has no body on earth but yours."

I think that's profoundly true. But I'd add this: we're also God's wombs.

Both the Jewish and Christian traditions affirm compassion as God's hallmark—a truth, by the way, that fire-and-brimstone preachers who turn religion into a bludgeon like to ignore. Throughout the Bible, in the Pentateuch, the Wisdom literature, the Prophets, the Gospels, and the Epistles, compassion is affirmed as the defining characteristic of God.

The word is derived from a Latin conjunction that literally means "to suffer with." So it makes sense that we tend to equate compassion with terms like "sympathy" and "fellow-feeling."

This identification isn't exactly wrong. But it doesn't go deeply enough.

*Rachamin* is the word for compassion found in Hebrew Scripture. It comes from *rechem*, or "womb." What Jesus and his Jewish ancestors meant by compassion was very much like the love of a mother for the children she carries and brings forth from her womb.

In other words, to say that God's chief characteristic is compassion is to say that God loves with the intensity and devotion of a mother.

We're so accustomed to using masculine pronouns when speaking of God that talk about divine maternal love can sit uneasily. But there are several explicit references to God's mother-love in the Bible.

In Genesis, God maternally broods over the void, like a hen over her eggs. In Deuteronomy, God hovers protectively over her hatchlings as a mother eagle does.

The prophets Isaiah and Hosea speak of God in maternal terms. God comforts us, proclaims Isaiah, as a mother comforts her children, giving them her breast to suckle. Hosea says that God protects us with the fierceness of a mother bear guarding her cubs.

Jesus compares his love for humans to that of a brooding hen—he surely intended to remind his hearers of the Genesis passage—and in one of his parables, he uses a steadfast woman as a metaphor for God's loving perseverance. In his multiple and generous healings, his refusal to indulge in snap judgmentalism, and his tender concern for society's down-and-outs, Jesus positively glowed with compassionate mother-love.

Many allusions to God as a loving mother are also found in the writings of mystics. One of the most striking comes from the fourteenth-century Dame Julian of Norwich. In her remarkable book *Showings*, she effortlessly and unselfconsciously refers to Jesus in both masculine and feminine terms, sometimes in the same sentence.

"As truly as God is our Father," writes Julian, "so truly is God our Mother." Jesus, she continues, "is our true Mother, in whom we are endlessly born." Just as a human "mother can give her child to suck of her milk, our precious Mother Jesus can feed us with himself."

Both the biblical and mystical traditions attest, then, that compassion is more than merely feeling the pain of others, important as that is. It's a state-of-soul and way-of-being that is life-bestowing and nourishing, persistent and patient, nonjudgmental and forgiving, fiercely protective and gently corrective.

Above all, compassion is a tender mother-love that joyfully and gratefully serves. This love obviously sympathizes or suffers when others suffer, but it does more than that. It strives to forestall or alleviate their pain and misery.

As Jesus said, what father—what mother—would offer a stone when his or her child asks for bread? The same goes for our divine father/mother. Which brings me back to the claim that you and I are God's wombs as well as God's eyes, hands, and feet. We carry within us God's likeness, and this means that the capacity for compassion is hardwired into our spiritual DNA. As disciples, we're summoned to give to our sisters and brothers a portion of the maternal love, the *rachamin*—that is, God's essential quality.

As God's eyes, we seek out people in spiritual and material want. As God's hands and feet, we labor to improve their lot. But as God's wombs, we're receptacles for the compassion, the mother-love, that sharpens our vision and animates our limbs in the first place.

# Grace-Mobbed

Theologians write learned books about grace. But when I think of it, what comes to mind is a flash mob.

If you ever witness one firsthand, you'll never forget it. You'll be in a bustling public place like a mall, surrounded by folks who, like you, are stressed out by the demands of everyday life. Suddenly, someone in the crowd will calmly take out a flute and begin playing. One by one, other musicians will emerge from the crowd with violins, cellos, and clarinets. Together they'll freeze time with music so beautiful and so unexpected that all you'll be able to do is stand and marvel.

Then, as suddenly as it began, it'll end. The performers will melt back into the anonymous crowd. The busyness of everyday life, temporarily suspended, will resume. Yet everything will be different, too.

A crowd's first response to a flash mob is surprise, and sometimes even confusion. But delight and joy quickly take their place, and by the time the performance is over, everyone is luminous with a sense of well-being. You can see it in their faces. Their lives, at least for a few moments, have been transported from the everyday here-and-now to a place of wonder and goodness. Something deep, something fundamental, has been touched.

This is exactly how grace works. In the Christian tradition, grace is an unexpected gift from God, lovingly bestowed for no other reason than to rejuvenate the recipient. The word is derived from the Greek *chairo*, which means "to be glad," "to rejoice," or "to be delighted." When we're seized by a grace moment—when we're grace-mobbed—it might take us by surprise. But then a surge of gladness, love, and hope lifts the curtain of our everyday lives just enough for us to catch a revitalizing glimpse of the fullness of creation, the beauty of humans, and the glory of God. When that happens, our faces glow. How could such a revelation not invigorate jaded hearts or inspire weary minds? How could we not be delighted?

# Grace-Mobbed

Back in the fourth century, Saint Augustine likened grace to a healing tonic. Too often, he pointed out, the busyness and minutiae of everyday life, not to mention its heartbreaks and tragedies, can get to us. Our spirits grow sluggish, our souls shut down, our imaginations go into hibernation. Like the injured wayfarer in the parable of the Good Samaritan, we need help to recover our sense of wonder and gratitude. We need to be grace-mobbed, and God, the Good Samaritan, obliges us.

The in-breaking of grace is everywhere. Grace abounds. It's encountered in the joy of love, the laughter of children, the beauty of the ocean, the kindness of a stranger, a good meal shared with friends, the softness of a summer night, the intimacy of lovemaking, the silence of prayer, the holiness of liturgy. Any situation, no matter how ordinary, can be a channel of grace. The Nag Hammadi scroll known as the Gospel of Thomas tells us that the world is shot through with it. "Split a piece of wood," Jesus says in the gospel, "and I am there. Lift a stone, and you'll find me."

Search just beneath the surface of the ordinary, and what you discover is the marvelous, the enchanted, the mysterious. You never know when musicians will step out of the crowd and transport you to a place of wonder and delight. You never know when the Divine will grace-mob you. As the poet Gerard Manley Hopkins vividly reminds us, "the grandeur of God, shining like shook foil," can be encountered anywhere.

The glorious thing about the gift of grace is that once it's received, it refuses to be contained. When we're grace-mobbed, the joy that we experience can't help but overflow, and we gift others with what God gave us. Grace emboldens us to love with abandoned profligacy, because grace opens our eyes to the sheer lovability of creation.

Some of us may try to resist grace, just as a curmudgeon might turn away from a flash mob with a sour "bah!" We may be too mired in the busyness of life, too swamped with everyday concerns, to allow it to open us up. But that's okay, because grace, like the Love that gifts it, is patient. Sooner or later, all of us get grace-mobbed.

# PART 3

# Being Good

# Nothing Is Permitted

Back in the sixteenth century, Francis Bacon offered some sage advice to readers. "Some books should be tasted and some devoured," he wrote, "but only a few should be chewed and digested thoroughly." One of the books most people would put in Bacon's third category is *The Brothers Karamazov*, written by the Russian novelist Fyodor Dostoevsky and published just two months before his death in 1881.

*Karamazov* is an exploration of the tension between faith and doubt that haunts but also enriches the human condition. Each of the brothers represents a point somewhere along a spectrum that runs from angry atheism to wild hedonism to ascetic saintliness. In the hands of a lesser author, such a theme could've devolved into bathos or finger-wagging preachiness. But Dostoevsky rose to the challenge.

One of the novel's more memorable lines, delivered by Dmitri, the hedonist brother, is this: "What will become of humans without God and immortal life? Are all things permitted then?" The insinuation is that, in the absence of a loving desire to please God and a hope of renewed life after death, there's no check on human behavior. A meaningless universe provides no incentive to behave morally.

Although I hesitate to disagree with Dostoevsky—I am, after all, a pigmy to his giant—I actually think that the absence of God creates a quite different dilemma. If God doesn't exist, it's nothing, rather than everything, which is permitted.

I take my cue from the nineteenth-century philosopher Friedrich Nietzsche, as bitter a foe of religion as the world has ever produced. In his book *The Gay Science*, he offers a chilling parable.

Residents of a certain town were amused one day to see a man carrying a lit lantern through the streets, even though it was high noon. When they asked him what he was up to, he told them he was looking for God.

The townspeople roared with laughter at this. "Has your God gone on vacation?" they jeered. "Is he perhaps taking his lunchbreak?" Angered by the taunts, the man dashed his lantern to the ground, pointed to a nearby church, and bellowed: "I'll tell you where God is—in that white sepulcher over there. God is dead—murdered by our indifference—and churches are now nothing but tombs!"

Don't misunderstand Nietzsche's parable. He celebrates rather than mourns deicide, believing as he does that most of the world's ills stem from religion in general and Christianity in particular. He longs for the day when humanity once and for all expunges the last shreds of God-belief from its collective psyche. Only then can women and men finally step out of the fog of faith into the light of reason.

Like Dostoevsky, Nietzsche believed that the erasure of God, the cultural loss of belief in a divine Lawgiver, destroys the foundation upon which humans have distinguished right from wrong for centuries. God's death deprives us of our customary moral compass. But whereas the Russian novelist sees this state of affairs as an ethical nightmare in which everything is permitted, the German philosopher, who proclaims that he wants to push humankind "beyond good and evil," applauds it.

But here's the problem. The ethical vacuum that the loss of a divine Lawgiver creates so disorients us that we no longer quite know what's good and what's evil. Consequently, any act we perform risks being immoral. But since we've slain God, we've also destroyed all hope of forgiveness, as Nietzsche himself admits. "What was holiest and mightiest of all that the world has yet owned has bled to death under our knives," he declares. "Who will wipe this blood off us?"

In a beyond-good-and-evil world, we may still use words like "redemption" or "forgiveness." But if God is dead, they're merely *flatus vocis*, windy words empty of content and signifying nothing.

And this brings me back to my disagreement with Dostoevsky. For the Nietzsches of the world, the death of God is a free pass for any kind of behavior, precisely the moral anarchy that Dostoevsky feared. But for the rest of us, God's disappearance more likely breeds a chronic state of moral uncertainty exacerbated by the despairing realization that there is no longer a chance of ultimate redemption. In such a horrible world, nothing is permitted because nothing is forgivable.

## Capital Punishment Is a Sin

I've always been struck by the fact that the gurneys on which we execute people are cruciform. Strapping condemned felons to these crosses of death is an obscene mockery of what happened on Golgotha.

It's also a sin.

There are plenty of practical and moral reasons to condemn the judicial killing of human beings. Data show that the threat of execution isn't an effective deterrent to murder, that capital sentences are handed out disproportionately to blacks, Latinos, and poor whites, and that it's more cost effective to imprison than to execute.

Moreover, there's no hard evidence that execution brings closure to the loved ones of murder victims. Finally, and shamefully, the United States is the only Western democracy that still puts people to death, thereby thumbing its nose at the Universal Declaration of Human Rights, earning Amnesty International's censure, and coarsening the national conscience.

Even if the facts were otherwise, however, followers of Christ would be obliged to oppose the death penalty. There may be occasions when killing is tragically unavoidable. An execution isn't one of them.

Christian defenders of capital punishment often try to justify their position by citing prooftexts from the Old Testament. It's true that there are some thirty-five offenses, including necromancy, idolatry, false prophecy, and bestiality, for which the Torah demands death.

But because defenders of execution who appeal to biblical teaching quietly ignore most of them, it's reasonable to presume that their position isn't quite as Bible-based as they pretend.

Regardless of what the Old Testament says, Jesus's teaching unambiguously rejects capital punishment. In the Sermon on the Mount, his single most significant discourse in the Christian Scriptures, Jesus repudiates the old eye-for-an-eye model of justice. Instead, he tells us to love our enemies and not to resist evildoers. This isn't a recommendation for passivity in the face of wickedness. The text's Greek verb *anthistemi*, usually translated as "to resist," actually means "to resist violently." So Jesus is telling us to reject a pseudo-justice that responds to violence with violence. He recommends restorative instead of retaliatory justice, and models it for us when he halts the public stoning of the adulteress.

The early church fathers took Jesus at his word. In the second century, Lactantius taught that Christians should never accuse anyone of a capital crime, arguing that it made no moral difference "whether a Christian puts someone to death by word or sword." His contemporary Origen agreed, as did Tertullian, who went so far as to insist that Christians shouldn't be civil magistrates lest they find themselves in the position of having to impose a capital sentence.

It wasn't until the fourth century, when Christianity was legally recognized and quickly became the de facto apologist for the Roman Empire, that the church dropped its condemnation of execution. Christianity in the American Empire also falls into line. 67 percent of white evangelicals and 59 percent of white Catholics support the death penalty. Not surprisingly, only a minority of black and Latino Christians do.

Christians who remain loyal to Jesus's rejection of capital punishment often appeal to a moral framework called the "seamless garment" or "consistent life" ethic. They argue that human life is sacred because it is imbued with the likeness of God, and thus should be honored and protected from womb to tomb. This perspective cuts across issues as diverse as abortion, capital punishment, warfare, care for the terminally ill, genetic engineering, political oppression, and systemic poverty.

A seamless garment approach to the death penalty holds that respect for life, even the life of a murderer, is owed to the Father who makes us, the Christ who liberates us, and the Holy Spirit who enlightens us. It doesn't in any way lessen compassion for victims whose well-being has been harmed by criminals, nor does it leave crimes unpunished.

The criminal who slays a person steals a life and pounds yet another nail into the crucified Christ's limbs. But if our justice system returns violence for violence by strapping offenders down on death gurneys, we compound the wickedness with which they've bespattered the world.

# Reclaiming Prudence

We live in a culture bent on keeping us in a permanent state of moral outrage. Shooting-from-the-hip judgmentalism is the order of the day. Accusations and condemnations get flung with abandon by politicians, pundits, talk radio hosts, social media trolls, and ordinary people like you and me. We can't seem to simply disagree with anyone anymore; instead, we demonize anyone who thinks differently than we do. Nor do we reserve our self-righteous anger for big ticket issues. Anything that rubs us the wrong way, no matter how slight, provokes our moral disapproval.

We badly need to reclaim the virtue of prudence.

Prudence is a word you rarely hear these days. That's a pity, because it names a virtue whose importance has been affirmed since antiquity. Without prudence, our moral compasses swing wildly. It's so essential to morality that it's called a "cardinal" virtue, from the Latin for "hinge." Prudence is the hinge on which all the other virtues turn.

Here's why. It does us no good to possess virtues such as, for example, courage or tolerance unless we know when it's appropriate to invoke them. Prudence is the ability, grounded in reason and experience, to discern what's morally fitting and what's not in a given situation. In its absence, a person who possesses the virtue of courage may misuse it by foolhardily rushing in where angels rightly fear to tread. Without prudence's guidance, the virtue of tolerance can wither into an indiscriminate permissiveness.

Prudence is crucial not only for making a sound moral judgment, but also for determining if one's even called for. There are plenty of behaviors and opinions we may dislike, but which it is rash to highhandedly condemn. One of the challenges of the moral life is discriminating between what merely sets our teeth on edge and what genuinely warrants ethical concern. Prudence helps us see that our discomfort with someone else's lifestyle or beliefs may not rise to the level of moral condemnation. People with whom we disagree usually aren't evil. They're just different.

All of us could benefit from exercising prudence. But I think Christians are especially in need of it because the stakes are so high when they question a person's behavior or beliefs. Christians don't just morally censure people they disapprove of. They call them sinners and consign them to the outer darkness until they repent. Moral condemnation doesn't get any heavier than this.

Now, I have absolutely no doubt that in fact there are behaviors and beliefs, private as well as corporate, that are sinful. But I'm equally convinced that much of what some Christians condemn as sin really isn't. Prudence would help them and the rest of us step away from our personal likes and dislikes long enough to distinguish between actions and beliefs that are genuinely culpable, and those that stick in our craws merely because they're different. The first should be deplored, but the second treated with forbearance.

Fifteen hundred years ago, Saint Augustine provided what just might be the best expression of religious prudence ever offered. Personally, I'd like to see it carved on the lintels of every church in the land. *In necessariis unitas, in dubiis libertas, in omnibus caritas*, he wrote. "Unity in necessary things; freedom in doubtful things; charity in all things." Pope Francis recently offered a shorthand version: "Who am I to judge?"

Too many Christians today ignore this sage counsel. They toss out imprudent judgments because they've mistaken what's merely *dubiis* for *necessariis*. They've become convinced that their faith requires them to issue angry condemnations of anyone with whom they personally disagree—gay couples, gay clerics, evolutionists, stem cell researchers, Muslims, atheists, and so on—and to sidebar the core of the very faith they profess: to walk in love as Christ loved us and gave himself for us. *In omnibus caritas* gets devoured by an Inquisition-like zeal to condemn.

In the absence of prudence, this take-no-prisoners harshness is predictable. Without prudence, the best of us—even the church—can lose a sense of moral direction and spin out of control.

So to everyone in our chronically angry culture, but especially to my fellow Christians, may I offer a bit of advice? Step back, take a few deep breaths, and pause before flying into holier-than-thou rages over issues that may not merit such energy. Be prudent. Focus on the essentials, and leave the rest to conscience and God.

# Against Moral Relativism

Anyone who's ever taught college-level philosophy, as I did for thirty-five years before chucking it in to become a fulltime priest, is all too familiar with the typical freshman's interpretation of morality. It goes like this: "If you think an action is good (or wicked), then it's good (or wicked) for you."

This response is the *bête noire* of philosophy professors because it's just about as hollow an opinion as a human being can hold. It confuses a tritely true and utterly uninformative observation—"if I think an action is good or wicked, then I think it's good or wicked"—with genuine moral analysis of whether an action is actually virtuous, independent of personal preference.

Its underlying and usually unarticulated assumption is that moral values are nothing more than personal/psychological or social/cultural artifacts, with no objective reality. The first is subjectivism, the second relativism.

This way of thinking about morality may be tolerable coming from green eighteen-year-olds, but it's inexcusable in mature adults. It's intellectually lazy, because even a tiny bit of mental effort reveals its bankruptcy; self-indulgent, because it potentially offers a faux justification for doing whatever one likes; and indecent, because it absolves us of the responsibility to call out wickedness in others. After all, if good and evil are simply matters of personal taste or social convention, live and let live.

But the truth of the matter, contrary to both subjectivism and relativism, is that we humans can't make something morally valuable merely by declaring that it is. This is as absurd, notes British ethicist John Cottingham, as presuming that we can "make coal nutritious by deciding to eat it." Instead, values such as love, compassion, justice, courage, loyalty, and truth exist independently of us. It is they who declare themselves to us, drawing us toward them. They are the inherently worthy pillars of human decency.

## Part 3: Being Good

If you doubt this because you're a subjectivist or relativist, ask yourself if you honestly think the moral status of what occurred on a Portland train in May 2017 is up for debate.

A man boarded the train, began shouting racist and xenophobic insults at two teenage girls (one of whom wore a hijab) and then viciously murdered two Good Samaritans who tried to intervene and wounded two others.

Shortly before he died from his injuries, one of the victims, twenty-three-year-old Taliesin Namkai-Meche, said, "I want everybody on the train to know, I love them." By contrast, his murderer, whose surname, jarringly, is Christian, said this when taken into custody: "Think I stab motherfuckers in the neck for fun? Oh yeah, you're right I do. I'm a patriot. I hope they all die. I'm gonna say that on the stand. I'm a patriot, and I hope everyone I stabbed died."

Every fiber of our being proclaims that the assailant's act was wicked, that the two girls were innocent, and that the Good Samaritans were righteous. Were someone to say, "well, yes, but the assailant thought his action was good; therefore, it was good for him," we'd be aghast at the remark's insensitivity.

Were someone else to say, "Well, perhaps in some cultures, Christian's action would be seen as good," we'd immediately respond that such a culture is morally suspect.

If we ran across someone who actually tried to insist that Christian's action was virtuous, we wouldn't say, "Okay, yes, I see your point. To each his own." We'd unhesitatingly reject such an opinion as shockingly off-base. That someone might view a heinous deed as either morally neutral or virtuous, no more provides an adequate argument against the objective reality of values than color blindness argues against color vision or deafness against hearing.

And that's all it takes. Once we grant the irrefutable wickedness or virtue of even one action, we call into question the banal claim that morality is nothing but a product of personal preference or historical accident. We can acknowledge that when it comes to making moral decisions in a complex and messy world, emotional preferences and cultural norms inevitably play a role. But to insist that they're the substance of morality is to let the tail wag the dog.

And in the Portland tragedy, it's to deflate both the evil that was perpetrated and the good that resisted it.

# Getting Clear on Conscience

In the 1940 Disney classic *Pinocchio*, Jiminy Cricket served up this bit of moral counsel in a catchy little tune: "When you get in trouble and you don't know right from wrong, give a little whistle! And always let your conscience be your guide!"

Super movie. Great song. But so-so moral advice unless we get clear on what conscience is.

Jiminy seems to think conscience is an infallible inner circle, a private moral compass that always points to true north. When confronted with a situation that calls for a moral decision, all we need do is listen to what this interior guide tells us. We'll know it's steered us in the proper direction when our choice "feels right."

But here's the problem. Two people facing the same moral dilemma can be led by their inner guides in utterly different directions. True north for one is dead south for the other. Think of the abortion standoff, or the debate over what to do with immigrants. Moreover, our inner guides can make horribly wicked acts "feel right," giving us a free moral pass to wreak havoc in the name of conscience. Think terrorists.

This suggests that the inner voice of conscience just isn't infallible. Any moral choice that "feels right" to us may be the product of confused reasoning, snap judgment, or self-serving rationalization. Feeling comfortable with a specific moral choice is no guarantee that it's the proper one. It doesn't take too many times around the block to learn that doing the right thing is often painful instead of warmly gratifying.

So Jiminy's advice to always let conscience be our guide needs some qualification. There has to be some standard, independent of personal preferences or emotions, to which conscience appeals. Otherwise, the inner voice is too subjective. In the Western democracies, we have a political right to freedom of conscience. But this doesn't mean that what passes for conscience is always morally right.

If conscience isn't a failsafe crystal ball that dispenses pop-up answers to specific questions, what is it? Anglican theologian John Macquarrie offers an intriguing alternative. The Greek and Latin words for "conscience," he reminds us, originally signified "awareness." Riffing off that, Macquarrie suggests that conscience is best understood as a special kind of awareness that reveals the gap between who we actually are and who we ought to be.

The distance between our actual and our ideal self can be measured by moral standards independent of personal preferences. The actual "me" falls ethically short of the ideal "me" whenever I fail to honor fundamental ethical principles that recommend compassion over cruelty, honesty over dishonesty, and fairness over inequity. When the moral gap between what I do and what I should do grows too wide, my conscience prods me to become a better person.

For persons of faith, the distance between the actual and the ideal "me" is measured, additionally, by how well we live up to our innate God-likeness. Judaism, Christianity, and Islam believe that humans are made in the image of a loving, wise, and just God. Hindus and Jains teach that there's a spark of the divine, the *atman*, in each of us. Buddhists believe that all persons possess a compassionate Buddha-nature.

In these religious traditions, the special awareness called conscience reminds us of our objective identity as children of God. It helps us remember that we're called by our very natures to imitate, as best we can, divine love, wisdom, and compassion. Conscience reorients us when sin or confusion causes us to lose our way. It summons us, as Jesus told his followers, "to be perfect as your Father in heaven is perfect" (Matt 5:48).

Ultimately, what we do in any given situation reflects what we want to be. Every moral decision we make points beyond itself to a more fundamental choice: will I strive to be my ideal self, or settle for my actual self? That's why conscience isn't simply in the business of telling us right from wrong whenever we whistle it up, much less a justification for personal preference. Instead, it's the deepest of calls, the profoundest summons, to live up to one's humanity and to one's nature as a child of God.

# Physician-Assisted Suicide

David Goodall, an Australian centenarian, made headlines in May 2018 by taking his own life in an act of physician-assisted suicide (PAS).

Although physically infirm because of his advanced age, Mr. Goodall suffered from no chronic or painful disease. He was simply tired of being old. So, insisting he had a right to decide when, where, and how to die, he chose to check out by means of a lethal injection.

It's not my place to morally judge him or anyone else who opts for PAS. I've been a pastor too long and witnessed too much end-of-life suffering for that. But I'm troubled by the model of human nature underlying most defenses of PAS.

Surveys show that only a thin margin of people who contemplate or actually request PAS do so because of chronic or debilitating pain. What primarily drives their choice is fear that age or illness will rob them of dignity, autonomy, and pleasure in life.

They fear their dignity will be lost if they have to rely on others for personal hygiene and bathroom needs. They fear their autonomy will be sacrificed if they're no longer able to do whatever they wish and go wherever they want. And they believe that death is preferable if activities they enjoy can't continue to life's end.

The understanding of human nature upon which these assumptions are based is what I call the "sovereignty of self" model. It sees human beings as creatures who are ruggedly individualistic, utterly self-sufficient, and uninhibitedly free to do whatever we choose.

Consequently, our dignity consists in swallowing pain, displaying no overt weakness, disdaining dependence on others, and living exactly and only as we wish. We are the sole masters of our fate and the exclusive captains of our souls. If we can no longer steer our own vessels, it's our indisputable right to scuttle them. Consequently, PAS is perfectly acceptable.

Although it's so ingrained in the American psyche that we might think it has a long pedigree, the sovereignty-of-self model is a relatively recent interpretation of what it means to be human. It arose from the eighteenth-century Enlightenment's embrace of the libertarian notions that humans are radically autonomous creatures bound to one another by nothing stronger than artificial social contracts, and that genuine human flourishing consists in self-sufficiency.

But this is completely antithetical to the Christian tradition—and, I would suggest, to any informed humanism, religious or otherwise.

In the Christian story, human dignity is inherent, a consequence of the fact that we're made in the image of God. Dependence on others that comes with sickness or age doesn't rob us of that dignity, any more than it robs dependent children of theirs, nor is it something that ought to shame us. Instead, it's an opportunity for the exercise of quintessential human qualities like humility and gratitude on our part, and love and compassion from those who tend to us.

Nor are we self-sufficiently autonomous. We're communal through-and-through. Far from being sovereign, our selves are interlocked in a vast web of mutual dependence. Christians express this by speaking of our inclusion in the body of Christ, that mystical communion with one another and God. But even most secularists acknowledge our profound interdependence when they refer to the "human family" or "global community."

Finally, quality of life isn't devastated when age or illness makes the activities we once enjoyed no longer possible. Life has different seasons. A wise person finds the meaning and pleasure appropriate to each of them instead of insisting, with arrested development stubbornness, that they all be cut from the same cloth. Life doesn't become unbearable if it ceases to be exactly what we want it to be.

So, peace to Mr. Goodall and to all who opt for PAS.

But that's not who we humans are.

# Moral Imagination

Given the incredible complexity of life, you'd think it wouldn't take too long for us to learn that determining what's morally right and wrong doesn't lend itself to formulaic responses. But never underestimate the human urge to avoid the hard work of navigating complex moral situations by falling back on one-size-fits-all bromides.

One of the most common ways that some religious people dodge the burden of moral navigation is simply to ignore the specifics of context and motive in situations that call for ethical decision-making. Instead, they fall back on dogmatic and unbending fidelity to a handful of abstract rules. Moral judgments are easy. Just mechanically invoke the rule and apply it across the board.

Champions of this approach hold it up as an exemplar of ethical and religious purity, a valiant refusal to kowtow to what they see as the anything-goes relativism of our corrupt age. But in fact it lacks an essential characteristic of authentic morality, something the eighteenth-century conservative philosopher Edmund Burke called the "moral imagination."

The moral imagination consists of "all of the superadded ideas, which the heart owns and the understanding ratifies, as necessary to cover the defects of our own naked shivering nature."[1]

Burke agreed that abstract principles such as the Golden Rule serve as objective guidelines for moral behavior. But applying them to the messy contexts and tangled human relationships of everyday life demands an interpretive finesse that, in sympathy with our "naked shivering nature," calls forth compassion, patience, forgiveness, and empathy. In the absence

---

1. Edmund Burke, *Reflections on the Revolution in France and Other Writings* (New York: Everyman's Library, 2015), 491.

of these "superadded ideas," abstract moral principles are blind, deaf, and potentially despotic.

Take the flashpoint issues of abortion and same-sex marriage, unequivocally condemned by many evangelicals and Roman Catholics as never, under any circumstance, morally acceptable. They justify their obduracy with mechanical appeals to abstract moral precepts that make no room for the "superadded ideas" required for authentic ethical judgment.

When it comes to abortion, the abstract precept that's invoked to condemn any and all terminations of pregnancy is the quite reasonable "all human life is precious." But no attention is paid to the particulars of a woman's situation—age, health, social status, circumstances of becoming pregnant, etc.—nor is there the slightest admission that early abortions just might carry a lesser moral weight than later ones.

Because such uncompromising opponents are blind, willfully or otherwise, to the gray moral zone in which many abortions fall, they have no time for the consideration of mitigating circumstances that might prompt compassion. They unimaginatively clutch at the precept that "all human life is precious" with no sensitivity to the inescapable fact that respecting the precept sometimes means making excruciating choices that fall somewhere short of moral perfection.

In morally condemning same-sex marriage, most Christian opponents content themselves with cherry-picking Scripture. The few who do struggle to offer a moral justification for their position generally invoke an "unnatural = immoral" precept, with the implication being that same-sex relations are unnatural.

Forget for the moment how difficult it is even to understand what we mean by the word "natural," which of course is always contextually slippery. (Magic was once considered "natural" and surgery "unnatural." Different times, different contexts, different meanings.) Let's pretend that we know what's natural. Let's furthermore allow, purely for the sake of the argument, that the unnatural is immoral and that same-sex relations are unnatural.

Moral imagination would ask us to consider whether it's decent to issue an across-the-board judgment that same-sex couples are incapable of loving commitment and wholesome family life. The "unnatural = immoral" precept notwithstanding, oughtn't the "superadded ideas" of tolerance and fellow-feeling play a role in our moral thinking about same-sex marriage—not to mention putting to rest the fiction that same-sex relations are somehow unnatural?

## Moral Imagination

Long before Burke coined the phrase, Jesus of Nazareth recommended and exhibited moral imagination. He forgave sinners, recognizing and commiserating with their "naked shivering nature." His two greatest parables, the Good Samaritan and the Prodigal Son, both advocate morally imaginative "superadded ideas" of compassion, love, and forgiveness instead of lockstep fidelity to rigid norms. Jesus the Christ knew that lockstep adherence to rigid moral principles isn't the same thing as a morally principled life.

The moral life, like the religious life, demands imaginative flexibility. We ignore reality, deny our better natures, and sin against others when fear, anger, or intolerance prompts us to pretend otherwise. All three inhibit moral imagination.

# Rehabilitating Shame

Two centuries ago, the poet William Blake complained of "priests in black gowns, walking their rounds, and binding with briars, my joys and desires."

I get his point. Too often over the last two millennia, Christ's call for moral rectitude has mutated into a dour, blue-nosed judgmentalism that condemns even the simplest and most innocent of human pleasures. The unhappy consequence is that many good people have been unnecessarily burdened with a crippling sense of shame.

So religion, if wielded as a censorious cudgel, can wreak havoc. When it does, many of its victims limp away forever. Egged on by a culture increasingly averse to emotional discomfort (more on this soon), a good number of them also repudiate the very concept of shame, dismissing it as an insidiously internalized mode of oppression. Shame, they conclude, is a feeling we're better off jettisoning.

Understandable as this response is, it's mistaken. Shame has value.

In ordinary language, most of us use the words "shame" and "guilt" interchangeably. But from an ethical perspective, they have different meanings. Guilt is a moral category, shame an emotional one. When we commit an evil act or refrain from a good one that we're capable of performing, we incur moral guilt or culpability. If we have a well-developed conscience, our misstep evokes shame in us.

A healthy sense of shame can also inhibit us from acting immorally in the first place. Additionally, we can feel shame on behalf of others who behave indecently, be they family members or presidential candidates.

So shame is an inner trigger or alarm of present or impending peril to moral character. We properly pay attention to signs such as nausea or fever that announce biological illness. Shame is a symptom of moral disorder, and we should heed it as mindfully as we do physical aches and pains.

That's why it's troublesome that we tend to repudiate unpleasant emotions such as shame, equating self-rebuke with unwholesome self-hatred, and criticism of our behavior by others as out-of-line judgmentalism. What originated as a legitimate rebellion against hyper-censorious religion has become an embedded cultural distaste for moral guilt and shame.

I'm afraid my generation, which came of age in the late sixties and early seventies, must shoulder a good deal of the responsibility for this state of affairs. We flower children rebelled against the "uptight" fifties culture of our parents, declaring ourselves liberated from the "guilt trips" they and the rest of society, including mainstream Christianity, tried to "lay on us." We wanted the space and freedom to "do our own thing."

Although most of us eventually packed away our tie-dye T-shirts, got jobs, moved to the suburbs, and settled into the very middle-class lifestyles we'd earlier despised, we couldn't quite let go of the belief that shame is unhealthy and ought to be avoided at all costs.

In banishing it, we also forsook the language of morality. Psychological terms replaced traditional ethical ones. Malefactors are troubled, come from unhappy homes, or are socially maladjusted through no fault of their own. The deeds they commit aren't evil so much as unfortunate, desperate, or self-destructive. Uneasy consciences are medicated instead of confessed. Shame is anesthetized with pills, therapy, and denial. I'm okay, you're okay.

It's not too much of a leap to see the uninhibited corruption of many corporate and political leaders in the years since, who all seem to have embraced Gordon Gekko's cinematic "Greed is good!" mantra, as one of the unhappy but utterly foreseeable consequences of our cultural rejection of shame.

Deny it as we might, shame is a valuable human response. Neither victims of religious puritanism nor cultural despisers of emotional discomfort should forget that. But it's important to keep Blake's poetic warning in mind. For a shamed response to be appropriate, there must be genuine, not contrived, guilt. Moreover, the shame must be proportionate to the guilt of the deed.

Just as hypochondriacs suffer from aches and pains where there is no physical illness, some neurotics are plagued by shame where there's no real moral guilt. Ethical as well as religious well-being requires getting clear about the proper boundaries of guilt and shame, and developing consciences capable of discerning them. But doing so requires renewed appreciation and rehabilitation of shame's moral value.

# Doing What Thou Wilt

They're a bit passé now, but there was a time when WWJD ("What Would Jesus Do?") bracelets were the rage. The letters, of course, were intended as a mnemonic nudge to imitate Jesus in thought and deed.

The problem is that most wearers of the bracelet strained their opinions about what it means to imitate Jesus through rightwing political and social filters. Their typical answers to "What would Jesus do?" included supporting the NRA, championing "family values," and denouncing "big government." Jesus, in short, became a Republican who expected his followers to be Republicans too. Not everyone who wore a WWJD bracelet subscribed to this wackiness. But enough did to discredit the whole movement

In place of the tainted WWJD mantra, I recommend LDWTW— "Love, and Do What Thou Wilt." Although a bit cumbersome, it's less exploitable by people who confuse their politics with their religion, and it has a longer pedigree than WWJD.

The expression that inspired the WWJD bracelets was coined in 1896 by Christian socialist Charles Sheldon. (I resist the temptation to dwell on the irony of conservative evangelicals embracing a leftist slogan.) "Love, and do what thou wilt" is from a fifth-century sermon preached by Saint Augustine.

Augustine's counsel may seem oddly latitudinarian, coming as it does from a guy who, in his *Confessions*, famously beat himself up for stealing some pears when he was a boy. But his "Love, and do what thou wilt" isn't at all the self-indulgent license that too often passes for love in our culture.

Unlike Augustine—and unlike the entire Western tradition, for that matter—we moderns tend to subjectivize love, first by reducing it to pleasurable feelings or emotions, and second by denying that it can be objectively defined or evaluated. This leads us to the inane conclusion that love is just whatever each person thinks it is, which in turn gives us permission to claim that any person, object, or act which gives us pleasure, no matter how frivolous or destructive it might be, is a candidate for lovability. In this witless context, "Love, and do what thou wilt" is as dangerous as a loaded gun in the hands of an imbecile.

But Augustine knew, as do all reasonable people, that love isn't always pleasurable. Sometimes, in fact, it can be a harsh and dreadful thing that obliges us to sacrifice ourselves for the good of others. Moreover, love isn't just whatever any person thinks it is. As Plato pointed out 2,500 years ago, the worthiness of love is objectively measurable in terms of how noble and good its object is. For Augustine, God is the epitome of nobility and goodness, and hence the proper ultimate object of our love. So when he says, "Love, and do what thou wilt," what he means is "Love *God*, and do what thou wilt." If we genuinely love God, we will naturally want to do only what is right in God's eyes. Love of God conforms our will to God's. Hence, "doing what thou wilt" parallels "doing what God wills."

But—and it's a big but—we have to be scrupulously honest about thinking through what God's will actually is. We can't allow our personal tastes, social biases, or political allegiances to cloud our judgment as they did in the WWJD craze. Instead, we must call upon reason, experience, and Scripture for the insight and integrity to ask tough questions about what's really important to God and what's not. Does God really care about sexuality more than about walking humbly, loving kindness, and doing justice? Can a nation that practices abortion, capital punishment, and euthanasia be genuinely righteous? Mustn't we sometimes break conventional rules to follow God's?

What, in short, is pleasing to God—not to our political party, our economic class, our ethnic or gender group, or our personal preferences—but to God?

Can we be so successful in conforming our will to God's that "doing what thou wilt" always falls into line with what God wants? Of course not. We are, after all, but human. But love gets us closer to the goal than WWJD chicanery. Love focuses us squarely on the Beloved instead of on pet projects and partisan loyalties that we fob off as God's. So retire your WWJD bracelet. Love God, who's neither a conservative nor a liberal, and then do what thou—and God—wilt.

# Our Sex-Obsessed Prophets

In his 2002 book *War Is a Force that Gives Us Meaning*, war correspondent Chris Hedges argued that there's something alluring about battle. Defying an enemy gives us a romantic sense of participating in a historic moment grander and more heroic than our day-to-day routines. It makes us feel as if our lives count for something.

There's also the adrenaline rush that comes from doing battle. As Hedges discovered in his years of frontline reporting, it can be pretty addictive.

I mention this because of the emergence in this country of certain Christians who, fancying themselves heirs to the Hebrew prophets, engage in spiritual warfare against what they see as a fallen and wicked culture. These men and women are in 24/7 battle mode. They and they alone hold the enemy at the gates. They and they alone defy the forces of evil. They and they alone have God's back.

What a rush it must be for these latter-day prophets! Not for them the mundane task of striving to be decent, ordinary Christians. That's too humdrum, too boring, and most of all, too anonymous. It's much headier to strap on the breastplate of righteousness, call in the press, and thunder jeremiads.

To riff on Hedges's title, waging raucous war against whatever they label as sin is a force that gives them meaning.

And what do these American-bred prophets find more wicked than anything else? Same-gender love and marriage. That's the fundamental sin shredding the moral fabric of society, dooming boatloads of people to hell, and causing the Almighty to look upon the nation with grave enough disfavor to punish it with natural disasters. To hear them, one would think that the apocalypse was ushered in by the 2015 Supreme Court decision legalizing gay marriage.

## Our Sex-Obsessed Prophets

The focus on sex by these crusaders is so obsessive that there's something suspiciously lurid about it—which, I suppose, only intensifies the battle-rush they already get from assailing the LGBT community.

Convinced though they may be that they're twenty-first-century successors to the Hebrew prophets, our homegrown sex-obsessed God-warriors are anything but.

The Hebrew prophets focused not on sex, but on two fundamental categories of sin: social injustice and religious hypocrisy. They urged the rich and powerful, including royalty and priests, to cease hoarding goods and privileges at the expense of everyone else. Moreover, they preached that what God desires from us is humility, love, and gratitude, and that no amount of formulistic ritual can make up for their absence.

True, the prophets often warned against "adultery." But they nearly never meant what their self-appointed American successors read into the word. For the Hebrew prophets, human infidelity to God, a violation of the sacred covenant or marriage between Yahweh and humanity, was an act of betrayal or adultery.

The real prophets of Judah and Israel, unlike the self-proclaimed ones of America, derived no romantic rush or self-glorifying smugness from their tasks. Moses, Isaiah, and Jeremiah all tried their best to squirm out of the summons. Amos pled he was unqualified for the job. Jonah fled God's call, winding up in the whale's belly for his pains. They all felt inadequate to what God asked of them. Such self-doubt, much less humility, is foreign to today's Christian prophets.

There's yet another crucial difference between then and now.

The Hebrew prophets were motivated by love of God, grief over oppression and religious hypocrisy, and a genuine desire to improve the lot of their people. True, they could get angry and speak harshly. But their anger wasn't fueled by hatred or contempt.

By contrast, the sex-obsessed denunciations of American prophets reek with disgusted scorn, even when they try to conceal their animosity behind cherry-picked Bible verses or theological arguments.

Hatred dressed up as piety is a force that gives them meaning.

Sexual morality is important. But it oughtn't to become our sole concern. In fact, from a biblical perspective, it's not nearly as urgent a worry as economic inequality or oppressive social and political practices. God, it seems, isn't as obsessed with sex as our pseudo-prophets are. They would do well to take to heart what God said to Ezekiel, a *real* prophet: "My hand will be against the prophets who see false visions and utter lying divinations."

# PART 4

# Culture and Community

# Weathering a New Dark Age

When we hear the word "renaissance," what comes to mind is the surge of art, music, science, and philosophy that erupted in Italy in the sixteenth century. Few of us remember its eighth-century predecessor, the Carolingian Renaissance, whose center was the court of Charlemagne and whose leading light was Alcuin of York, described by one of his contemporaries as the most learned person of his generation.

Europe was in bad shape in the eighth century, sunk in a period that historians call the Dark Age. Illiteracy was the norm—even priests and monks who painstakingly copied manuscripts were rarely able to read them—schools were practically nonexistent, and Latin and Greek classics lay untouched on monastic shelves.

Under the rule of Charlemagne, things changed. He gathered scholars from all over Europe to bring about a great revival of learning ably supervised by Alcuin. Schools were founded, textbooks were written, priests were better educated, and classical masterpieces were at risk of vanishing from memory rescued, studied, and remembered.

To encourage literacy, copyists in the Carolingian Renaissance even invented a more legible script that, unlike Roman block lettering, included lower and uppercase letters and punctuation.

Alcuin and his fellow scholars believed it their duty to weather the barbarism engulfing Europe by rescuing at-risk Latin classics and revitalizing Christianity. Their hope was that the rich legacy of pagan and Christian learning from earlier times could be preserved and passed on to future generations once the darkness lifted.

Thanks to them, large pieces of the Western canon survived, but it was touch and go. As art historian Kenneth Clark once observed, Western civilization just managed to hang on by the skin of its teeth.

## Part 4: Culture and Community

Several commentators today have suggested that the northern hemisphere is entering into a New Dark Age. They believe our accelerating slide into darkness is evidenced by the growing wealth gap, inept or corrupt political leadership, cynicism, the substitution of effortlessly gleaned cyber information for reflective thought, instant-gratification consumerism, frenetic hedonism, ethnic and religious violence, and moral relativism.

The most troubling sign of our New Dark Age is the crumbling of the Christian ethos that inspired many of the West's greatest artistic, literary, philosophical, ethical, and even scientific achievements. Today, Christianity in Europe and North America is moribund, beaten down by the steady pummeling of post-Enlightenment scorn but even more seriously wounded by post-modernity's yawning indifference to religion. Most mainline denominations, if the steady hemorrhage of their members is any indication, are clueless about how to halt Christianity's death throes, and too exhausted to do so even if they knew how.

Nor are media-savvy televangelists, cool hipster preachers who flaunt tattoos and body piercings and drop f-bombs, or defiantly irrational Christian fundamentalists hopeful signs of rejuvenation. Far from being pockets of resistance to the descending darkness, they're actually its whelps.

The future predicted by poet William Butler Yeats's prophecy in his "The Second Coming"—"the darkness drops again, things fall apart; the center cannot hold; mere anarchy is loosed upon the world"—is drawing nearer.

If those of us who remain loyal to Christianity hope to see its good news weather the descending darkness, we have to face the challenging truth that it is up to us to preserve what we can of it. We must let the example of Alcuin inspire us to do in our own day what he did in his: collect, protect, and pass on to future generations a precious legacy in danger of being forgotten.

His primary task was preservation. So is ours.

To succeed, we must hunker down in smaller faith communities that hold fast to the heart of Christian doctrine and morality. We must discipline ourselves to forgo our parochial squabbling and focus instead on our shared theological, philosophical, and moral convictions. We must enter ever more deeply into prayer, Scripture, and tradition, and remember that we belong first to Christ and only second to the nation in which we dwell. In whatever we do, we must suborn our personal ambitions to the greater call of living and preserving the faith handed down to us.

If we succeed, the New Dark Age won't be entirely dark, and dawn, however distant, remains a hope. If we fail—or, even worse, don't even try—night descends and darkness reigns.

# All Sheep, No Goats

We live in a time and place that seethes with tribal rage and fear.
Political rivalry is the fiercest it's been in my lifetime, with reds and blues quivering with such loathing for one another that they're unwilling to be in the same room.

Racism has slithered up from the sewer, where it lurked for a few years, to unabashedly chant its hateful slogans in the streets and scrawl them on walls.

Culture warriors, each camp despising the other with frightening intensity, battle acrimoniously over sexual mores as if the world's fate depends on the outcome.

Many Christians self-righteously bash Muslims, not to mention other Christians with whom they disagree, and Muslim extremists bash everything non-Muslim. Buddhists kill Hindus, Hindus kill Muslims, atheists verbally attack believers, and anti-Semitism is on the rise.

In short, we now think in binary terms. We divide the world into "us" and "them," sheep and goats. The insightful cultural observer Rabbi Jonathan Sacks calls this "pathological dualism." It's a sickly distorted way of looking at the world because humans simply aren't one-dimensional. No person is exclusively good or bad.

Pathological dualism gives rise, says Sacks, to "altruistic evil," the view that "we," who have right and justice on our side, are justified in assailing the unholy and wicked "them." This kind of thinking spawns a crusader mentality that bestows pseudo-moral permission to do horrible things to "them."

Even though Jesus warned against self-righteously dividing the world into sheep and goats—"Judge not, that you be not judged"—too many of us who claim to follow him have failed to heed his counsel.

## All Sheep, No Goats

But one person who took him seriously was the third-century theologian Origen. Origen learned firsthand about the danger of pathological dualism while still a lad in the city of Alexandria, when his father and hundreds of other "evil" Christians were slaughtered in an officially sanctioned pogrom. Later, as a priest and theologian, he personally experienced its effects when he was imprisoned and tortured by "righteous" Christians who accused him of heresy.

In light of his own experiences, as well as his fidelity to Christ's message, Origen denied that people can ever properly be judged utterly evil and totally condemned, and he did so in a theologically radical way: he defended universalism, the belief that no one, neither humans nor demons, will be consigned to permanent hellish darkness. Everyone capable of sin will ultimately be saved. Salvation is universal. At the end of the day, there are no goats, but only sheep.

The obvious ethical implication is that if God forgives everyone, humans have no justification whatsoever for condemning one another in a once-and-for-all way.

Origen spelled out his case for universalism in his book *On First Principles*. His argument is that no one made in God's likeness is capable of total corruption. Consequently, all humans and fallen angels, no matter how much evil they may commit, will eventually remember who they are and embrace the God from whom they came.

True, it may take some longer than others. Some, wrote Origen, will "outstrip others, and tend by a swifter course towards perfection, while others follow close at hand, and some a long way behind." But given enough time—and God is infinitely patient—everyone, even Satan, will be redeemed.

Ironically, Origen was persecuted as a goat precisely because of his refusal to divide the human race into sheep and goats. Most of his books were burned to silence him—an act of altruistic evil which its perpetrators justified by claiming that his writings corrupted unwary readers. But Origen's central message survived: if no one is beyond God's redemption, who are we to judge and unequivocally condemn our sisters and brothers?

That's a question we Christians today really need to take seriously.

# Breathing in Hiroshima

August 6 and August 9 are solemn days, marking as they do the first and, thanks be to God, only wartime use—so far—of nuclear weapons.

Although the term wasn't around in 1945 when atomic blasts destroyed Hiroshima and Nagasaki, the two bombs surreally named "Little Boy" and "Fat Man" were genuine weapons of mass destruction. When they exploded over their targets, a quarter-million people instantly vaporized. Tens of thousands more perished later from wounds, radiation sickness, and radiation-induced cancer and birth defects. All this carnage from two bombs whose killing power, when compared to today's nuclear weapons, was really quite modest.

Although they should be two of the most remembered days of the year, days in which we mourn all victims of war and honor them by resolving to turn our swords into plowshares, the anniversaries of Hiroshima and Nagasaki increasingly pass unobserved, at least in this country. When they actually are noted, they too often get hijacked by liberal and conservative pundits squabbling over whether dropping the bombs was a military necessity. The heat of these ideological feuds can easily distract us from a full appreciation of the savage enormity of destruction wrought by the two blasts.

We tend to be unmindful of the anniversaries for temporal as well as spatial reasons. Our historical memory is short. The bombings were seventy years ago, and most Americans who were alive in 1945, and who could help keep the memory of Hiroshima and Nagasaki fresh, are gone. Moreover, the two atomic blasts exploded on the other side of the world, far away from North America in both distance and culture.

Perhaps we would be more aware of the two anniversaries if we stopped to consider that they're actually much closer to us than we think. It's entirely likely that at some time or other in our lives, we've all breathed in airborne particulates of the two cities' vaporized victims. The mushroom clouds that rose over Hiroshima and Nagasaki hurled human flotsam and jetsam skyward. Winds then carried the dust around the globe, so that we who live inhale a bit of cruel death. The suffering of 250,000 of our sisters and brothers is, in a very real way, part of us.

But so are all their joys. As a wise friend recently reminded me, when we breathe in the dust of Hiroshima and Nagasaki victims, we also absorb their loves, their dreams, and their goodness. We inhale children who laughed at play, parents who adored their kids, lovers who felt fulfilled in one another's arms, and young scholars who dreamt of going to university. These too become part of who we are.

The larger point suggested by our literal inhalation of Hiroshima and Nagasaki victims is that each and every human being on the face of the earth is intimately and inextricably linked to everyone else. As John Donne famously noted, no person is an island. We share the same air, tread on the same earth, have the same basic human experiences. This isn't just because we're all members of the same biological species. More fundamentally, it's because we're tied together spiritually. We're siblings who share the same divine Parent.

The Christian expresses this unbreakable kinship in terms of the "body of Christ," and the Buddhist expresses it through the notion of "inter-being." But both Christians and Buddhists believe that when some of us suffer, all of us feel—or would, if we were mindful—a ripple of pain. Likewise, when others of us rejoice, we all—or at least should—feel their happiness.

Whether we acknowledge it or not, every second of the day, with each breath we take, we inhale all humans who have ever lived. We take in the pains and the joys of all humankind, and humankind in turn is sustained by the breath, the spirit, the *pneuma*, of God.

It's good to set aside certain days to recollect our deep bond with all other humans, as well as, for those of us who are religious, our shared dependence on God. The anniversaries of the nuclear nightmare that fell upon our Japanese sisters and brothers in 1945 offers us that opportunity. In honoring their memory, we embrace them as kin, we listen deeply to their stories, and we resolve to do better.

# When Darkness Descends

I've been thinking a lot lately about the biblical story in Exodus of the plagues that befell Egypt when its hard-hearted pharaoh refused to treat the Israelites as the human beings they were.

I think there just may be a lesson in it for us today.

Pharaoh viewed the Israelites as aliens, outsiders who were risks to national security, even though they had lived peacefully in Egypt for generations and were a numerical minority. So, to keep them in line, he enslaved them and even ordered all their male infants slain. The great liberator Moses just barely escaped this fate.

Pharaoh also disdained the Israelites as noxious drains on the system, even though they mixed, molded, stacked, and carried tons of bricks for the empire—bricks, I suppose, that built many a barrier wall. The truth is that they contributed much more to the Egyptian economy than they ever received.

But never mind. When you despise a group of people simply because they don't belong to your particular cultural, ethnic, or religious tribe—when you reduce them to subhuman status by denying them the basic rights that all persons deserve—facts tend to go limp and get replaced by "alternative" ones.

Exodus tells us that Yahweh, taking pity on the Israelites, anointed Moses to lead them out of bondage. Pharaoh refused to let them go, whereupon plague after plague beset him and the entire land of Egypt until he finally relented.

From our perspective, some of the plagues come across as more annoying than frightening. It's a drag to be ankle-deep in frogs or bedeviled by head-circling gnats, but it's hardly what you'd call FEMA out for. Subsequent plagues—painful boils, destroyed crops, diseased herds—were much more serious. And then, horribly, there was the plague crescendo, the death of the firstborn in every Egyptian household, a tragedy that mirrored Pharaoh's slaying of male Israelite infants.

Terrible as this final affliction was, it's the ninth plague, the one immediately preceding it, that haunts me. "Then the Lord said to Moses, 'Stretch out your hand toward heaven that there may be darkness over the land of Egypt, a darkness to be felt.'"

Biblical commentators interested in finding natural causes for the Egyptian plagues often contend that this one must have been caused by a sandstorm that blocked out the sun and stung unprotected flesh. But to reduce the ninth plague to a mere natural phenomenon strikes me as an impoverished reading of it.

It was a darkness of moral failing and spiritual corruption, not of wind and sand.

There are certain periods in human history when a moral darkness descends, and its corrosive effects become palpable—a thick, cloying "darkness to be felt"—both personally and socially. These are the times in which we forget (or, even worse, deliberately discard) common standards of decency that we once honored. We dim the light of reason and goodness, and dwell in the murk that spawns irrationality and cruelty.

Both the Hebrew and Christian Scriptures are pretty clear about what those standards are. They include hospitality to the stranger, compassion for society's most vulnerable, avoidance of the pitfalls of greed, jealousy, anger, arrogance, and vituperation, an irenic spirit that seeks dialogue instead of conflict, brotherly and sisterly love, and respect for the God-implanted dignity of each and every human being.

Moral darkness descends upon the land when we allow fear, prejudice, moral indifference, timid acquiescence, and self-centeredness to get the upper hand. Once the darkness falls, it becomes progressively harder to find one's bearings, and much easier to become so morally disoriented that conscience shuts down. As Proverbs says, where there is no vision—when a moral climate of fear and paranoia darkens the heart's eyes—the people perish.

Pharaoh and his people lived in moral darkness for years by the time Yahweh called Moses to deliver the Israelites. Perhaps the penultimate plague was a push on God's part to jolt Egypt into the recognition that for too long she had condoned oppression in the name of national security and embraced a caste system that rejected "outsiders" as prima facie inferior, dangerous, and contemptible.

## Part 4: Culture and Community

Pharaoh was too far gone in his moral blindness to heed God's warning all those centuries ago, and his hard-hearted arrogance was his undoing. Like I said: a lesson for us today.

# Whitewashing the Faith

"The church is still the most segregated major institution in America. At 11:00 on Sunday morning, when we stand and sing that Christ has no east or west, we stand at the most segregated hour in this nation."

So said Martin Luther King Jr., fifty years ago. It was true then and still is today. A 2018 LifeWay Research survey revealed that 81 percent of American Protestant congregations are either predominantly white or predominantly African American. Roman Catholic congregations tend to be a bit more integrated.[1] But as theologian Fr. Bryan Massingale puts it, "whiteness" is "normative" in the American Catholic experience.[2]

There are many reasons for the segregation of American churches. One of the more obvious ones is the unhappy fact that we white Christians are no more immune to the sin of racism than white Americans in general. This means, minimally, that we seldom go out of our way to make it easy for African Americans to worship with us. For their part, African Americans quite understandably feel more comfortable in predominantly black congregations where Christianity isn't so relentlessly white.

I was reminded of all this recently while watching "I Am Not Your Negro," a 2016 documentary about James Baldwin, the African American author who died in 1987. Baldwin spent his entire adult life battling racism. Although the film doesn't do the fact justice, much of his crusade was fueled by an angry sense that he and other African Americans had been betrayed by a normatively white Christianity.

---

1. LifeWay Research, "Protestant Pastors Want Churches to be Diverse, See Slow Progress," https://lifewayresearch.com/2018/03/20/protestant-pastors-want-churches-to-be-diverse-see-slow-progress/, para. 3.

2. Brian N. Massingale, *Racial Justice and the Catholic Church* (Maryknoll: Orbis, 2010), 23.

## Part 4: Culture and Community

Born in Harlem, the young Baldwin quickly discovered that he needed to belong to some kind of group to protect himself from street gangs on the one hand and police harassment on the other. So he joined one of the many storefront Pentecostal churches in his neighborhood, and shortly afterwards, at the age of fourteen, had an intense conversion experience. For the next three years, confident that he was sanctified by the blood of the Lamb, Baldwin was a fiery and apparently mesmerizing street preacher.

By the time he reached his late teens, however, he decided that remaining in the church was morally impossible. Baldwin left, he said, to become "an honest man." Years later, in his collection of essays entitled *The Fire Next Time*, he reflected on why he forsook Christianity.

As a black man, he wrote, he necessarily lived in a universe which had "evolved no terms for [his] existence." (African-American novelist Ralph Ellison made the same point by claiming that, in a normatively white world, blacks were invisible.) To cope with his sense of abandonment, the young Baldwin had turned to God. "But God," he soon discovered, "is white. And if His love was so great, and if He loved all His children, why were we, the blacks, cast down so far?"[3]

When he wrote this, Baldwin had ceased to believe that God exists. So his point was that white American Christians failed to walk their talk of brotherly and sisterly love, either simply disregarding all their Sunday-school rhetoric about compassion and mercy, or cynically distorting it to ignore or even exclude black persons. They relegated blacks to second-class spiritual status, and African Americans who embraced mainstream Christianity inevitably risked internalizing a deep sense of inferiority.

Moreover, to Baldwin's mind, membership in all-black congregations did nothing to mitigate the damage. By advocating Christian "virtues" of meekness and forbearance, black clergy encouraged a passivity in their parishioners that actually acquiesced to American Christianity's—not to mention the overall culture's—default standard of whiteness.

Such a situation Baldwin found intolerable. Consequently, he concluded that to be a "truly moral human being" it was necessary to "divorce" himself from "all the prohibitions, crimes, and hypocrisies of the Christian church." The concept of God, he insisted, was only useful if it made people "larger, freer, and more loving. If God cannot do this, then it is time we got rid of Him."

---

3. James Baldwin, *The Fire Next Time* (New York: Modern Library, 1995), 30.

Baldwin's rejection of what he disdainfully called "this white God business" is a disturbing reminder of how easy it is for white American Christians to make whiteness the spiritual norm. Until we come to terms with that, churches will remain segregated and the body of Christ will suffer.

# The Jesus Line

In J. R. R. Tolkien's magnificent Christian allegory *The Lord of the Rings*, a somber Gandalf tells Frodo that the Dark Lord has returned and is on the move.

"I wish it need not have happened in my time," says Frodo.

"So do I," Gandalf responds, "and so do all who live to see such times. But that is not for them to decide. All we have to decide is what to do with the time that is given us."

I feel much like Frodo these days, bewildered and frightened by the darkness descending upon the land.

The obscene gap between have and have-nots continues to widen; the environment is gutted by rapacious oligarchs and politicians; desperate refugees are met with suspicious hostility; access to affordable health care is relentlessly attacked; hate crime against religious and ethnic groups is skyrocketing; the national war machine is revamped to the tune of billions of dollars; foreign dictators who disdain human rights are courted; and mean-spirited incivility, rage, recrimination, mockery, and outright duplicity dominate public discourse.

Like Frodo, I wish the times were less toxic. But they aren't. So, as Gandalf pointed out, the only choice is to decide what to do with the time in which we find ourselves.

We Christians know how we're supposed to respond, even if we don't always act accordingly. We're called, as Saint Paul wrote, to be "ambassadors for Christ, as though God were making his appeal through us." At all times, but especially in dark ones like these, our duty is to convey through word and deed the message of the God we worship. Retreat or withdrawal, although tempting, simply isn't an option. Doing so betrays the incarnational God-in-the-world core of our faith.

## The Jesus Line

Contrary to what many American Christians think, being a faithful ambassador for Christ definitely doesn't mean obsessing over sexual morality, as if that's God's only concern.

Instead, it's to emulate Jesus by feeling compassion for and ministering to the socially marginalized, be they native daughters and sons or foreigners who seek asylum from oppression. Representing Christ means respecting the God-bestowed dignity of all human beings, and affirming the rights which are theirs by virtue of their humanity. It means cherishing the beauty and goodness of the earth given us by a beneficent God rather than greedily and wantonly ravaging it and its creatures. It requires us to resist the arrogance, anger, and shallowness currently poisoning our cultural and political climate by modeling the virtues of patience, forbearance, compassion, humility, and hope. And it obliges us to muster the courage to defy both political and religious leaders when their actions and words bolster rather than counteract the poison.

Our faith isn't just another species of political activism or social reform. We should never conflate partisan politics with Christ's message. Yet as ambassadors for Christ, we may be forced by the time in which we live to express our allegiance to him through political activism and social reform, as well as personal behavior, laboring for a society (as Catholic Worker founder Dorothy Day said) in which it's a bit easier for people to be good.

This of course doesn't mean that we embrace violent rabble-rousing or gratuitous trouble-making. We should respect political authority whenever it comports itself properly. Jesus himself tells us to render to Caesar what is Caesar's. But his intent in doing so was to warn against passively acquiescing to Caesar overstepping his bounds. When that kind of abuse occurs, we must resist, as Jesus did, or risk betraying our calling.

For Christians, then, there is definitely a line—call it "the Jesus line"—which we can't cross if we hope to retain our identities as Christ's ambassadors. That line is defined by the Sermon on the Mount; the compassion, mercy, hospitality, and love Jesus offered the dispossessed and scorned social pariahs he encountered; his humble but firm defiance of temple and state abuses of power; and the thirst for justice and common decency that Jesus inherited from the Hebraic prophetic tradition.

We Christians cross the Jesus line when we fail or, even worse, refuse to be stalwart ambassadors in the times that have been given us. Jesus said, "If you love me, you will keep my commandments." It's pretty clear, despite obfuscations by those who put politics before faith, what that means.

# Golden Rule Justice

What most of us have in mind when we hear the word "justice" is crime and punishment. But in his 1971 landmark *A Theory of Justice*, philosopher John Rawls was more interested in distributive or social justice: the fair allocation of resources and opportunities.

In his book, Rawls offered a now-famous thought experiment he called the "veil of ignorance." Consider, he wrote, what kind of society you'd want to live in if you knew nothing about your personal situation except that you lived in community with others. Once you step behind this veil of ignorance, you forget your religion, gender, social status, health, ethnicity, talents and weaknesses, income level, and education. Then, stripped of all knowledge about your present station in life, thereby maximizing objectivity and minimizing personal bias, what would a just society look like to you?

Rawls argues that those of us behind the veil most likely would come to the rationally self-interested conclusion that equality of opportunity and equitable distribution of resources would be the most just model.

Additionally, rational self-interest would dictate the importance of safety nets for people who fall on hard times or are unable to care for themselves. After all, any of us could wind up being one of society's down-and-outs. So when it comes to the least privileged members of society, exceptions to the general rule of equitable distribution are legitimate. Justice dictates that they ought to be given extra resources and opportunities to help them achieve parity with the rest of us.

The legacy of Christianity is so embedded in Western culture that even those who have no faith often unwittingly think in Christian-like frameworks. Although he'd once considered becoming an Episcopal priest, the trauma of World War II shattered Rawls's belief in God. But an echo of his youthful religion came out years afterward, because his veil of ignorance thought experiment is clearly a version of Jesus's Golden Rule to do as you would be done by. If I want society to treat me justly, I should want as much for everyone else.

Rawls's secular adaptation of the Golden Rule rests on rational self-interest. But as we all know from sad personal experience, "rational" self-interest easily mutates into "rationalized" self-interest, in which we contrive faux-ethical justifications for doing whatever we want.

Jesus's Golden Rule doesn't have the same problem because its center of gravity is humble, loving, and sometimes sacrificial service to others, not egoistic self-interest. The entire Sermon on the Mount, the text in which Jesus gives us the Golden Rule, focuses on how we humans can forsake our ego-selves and grow into our ideal-selves, the ones God intends us to be.

What's required is a steady renunciation of self-interest and an embrace of the poverty of spirit that enables us to turn the other cheek, cease our judgmentalism, love our enemies, and refrain from illicit pleasures. We're to chip away at our me-centered universes so that eventually, as Saint Paul says, it is Christ, not our petty and greedy egos, who lives in and motivates us. This Christ-self is our ideal self.

In giving us the Golden Rule, Jesus provides a firm foundation for justice. It's only when we treat others with the unconditional love that springs from the Christ-self that economic inequality, oppression, and bondage will be eradicated.

Moreover, our loving treatment of others aids them to make contact with their own Christ-selves. The Christ-self in us reaches out into the as yet hidden Christ-self in them, so that they too might escape the clutches of ego and live more abundantly. And once that happens, the circle of justice of Christ's unconditional love expands.

Rawlsian self-interest can't do this. That's because the ego-self is a bundle of desires that, if not disciplined, enslaves us. If the insatiable ego-self treated others as it wished to be treated, we'd be indulging our own worst character traits and encouraging wickedness in others. "Treating others as I wish to be treated" would always focus on the "I wish."

But when Christ lives in us, "treating others" takes precedence. We long for their fair treatment and their spiritual and material flourishing, not out of self-interest but out of unconditional Christ-love. This Golden Rule justice is what we'd want for ourselves, it's what we should want for others, and it's what God wants for everyone.

# Democratizing Evil

The observation that a cloud of angry mistrust has descended upon this nation is so obvious as to be banal. Political partisanship has never, at least in my lifetime, been so bellicose. Vile expressions of racial and ethnic hatred are on the upswing. Simmering fury is hair-triggered to explode at the slightest provocation.

Even the practice of Christianity, about which more and more Americans, despite protestations to the contrary, are indifferent, has been infected by this toxic mood. In the hands of politically partisan zealots, God has become a yes-man who obligingly endorses policy, and the faith has been fashioned into a bludgeon to intimidate anyone who wanders from the party line.

One of the most provocative and brilliant theologians of the twentieth century, Jacques Ellul, presciently diagnosed the malaise that's overtaken us. He called it the "democratization of evil."

Ellul noted with alarm the increase in widespread evil that began during his lifetime. (He died in 1994.) It wasn't, he argued, that individuals were becoming more immoral. "To be sure, people [today] are no worse than those in past centuries." But we're no better either, and the problem is that we "now have more powerful agents at [our] disposal." As a consequence, the damage that we can inflict on others, and on the planet itself, is more far-reaching than in earlier times.

For millennia, wrote Ellul, major evil for the most part was perpetrated by a small percentage of secular and religious rulers and aristocrats in whose hands unchecked power was concentrated. But no more. As wealth has spread more evenly and standards of living have improved, "instruments that can hurt our neighbors or unknown people" have become widely distributed.

In this new world order, you don't have to be a potentate to create discord. Evil is no longer the prerogative solely of the powerful.

## Democratizing Evil

Because Ellul wrote about the democratization of evil in 1989, some of the examples he used to illustrate his thesis might strike us as quaint today. He cites, for example, noise and automobiles as weapons of democratized evil, the first as a ubiquitous destroyer of tranquility and the second as encouragers of "vanity, scorn, competition, and anger."

And yet we ought not dismiss these two examples as pet peeves of an aging curmudgeon. Hard experience teaches us that any rock and roller with a sound system can assault an entire street block, and any yahoo with a drivers license can become a road-rage warrior.

Pollution is a more dramatic consequence of the democratization of evil, "the result of power placed in the hands of almost all citizens" to indulge in thoughtless consumption and casual discarding. Ellul died before global warming became the horrific reality it is today. But were he alive, he would name it for what it is: an evil created not only by a handful of profit-greedy corporations, but also by millions and millions of commodity-greedy consumers.

In other words, by we, the people.

Ellul also died before the appearance of the most potent democratizer of evil to date: social media.

Individuals throughout the world now have the extraordinary power, simply by hitting a few keys on a computer or smartphone, to spew unfiltered hatred and disinformation to a virtual global audience. Reasoned political discourse has been hijacked by a 280-character mode of communication. Genuine religious dialogue has been replaced by fanatical ranting on Facebook and electronic bulletin boards.

Even when we're not actually on our smartphones, many of us have so internalized social media's abbreviated and shallowly judgmental style that we remain locked in social media mode.

How do we halt the democratization of evil? Ellul is clear that attempting to impose some kind of external moral order, as many Christians who have succumbed to political partisanship advocate, won't work. Such efforts, ironically, serve only to disseminate even more widely the evil they claim to be combating.

What's needed, argues Ellul, is "to find the way of self-mastery, of respect for others, of a moderate use of the powers at our disposal."[1] For all of

---

1. Jacques Ellul, *Essential Spiritual Writings*, ed. Jacob E. Van Vleet (Maryknoll: Orbis, 2016), 115.

us, religious or otherwise, this demands a return to simple decency, regardless of political affiliation. For Christians, it means putting faith before flag.

Hopefully, we'll take Ellul's recommendation to heart before the evil we're democratizing becomes so overwhelming that there's no way back.

# Christian Nation Basics

Members of the Christian Right loudly and frequently proclaim that the United States is a "Christian nation." I've never quite grasped what they mean by that phrase.

That the founders were Christian? Some were, but many weren't, and some, like George Washington, were only nominally Christian.

That the founders frequently invoked the Christian God in their private correspondence and diaries? Again, some did, many didn't. That Christian commitment is written into our founding documents? Nope. Thomas Jefferson, who authored the Declaration of Independence, most emphatically wasn't a Christian, and the Declaration's "Creator" is the Enlightenment God of deism, not Christianity. And the only mention of God in the Constitution is in the document's date: "in the year of our Lord 1787."

That most colonists in 1776 claimed to be Christian? But what kind of Christian? Calvinist? Quaker? Roman Catholic? Baptist? Anglican? Anabaptist? It makes a difference. A Baptist nation would look pretty different than a Catholic one. And why, anyway, would a nation be Christian simply because most of its white inhabitants were two centuries ago?

So, to figure out just what makes a nation Christian, I turned to Christianity's own founding documents, the Old and New Testaments of the Bible.

Here's what I discovered. In a Christian nation:

- We would cherish and protect the environment because it's the good handiwork of God and because God appointed us its stewards (Gen 1:1–14, 28).
- We would revere human life from womb to tomb, knowing that each person is made in the likeness of God (Gen 1:27).

## Part 4: Culture and Community

- Immigrants would be welcomed (Exod 22:21–24).
- Usury wouldn't be practiced (Exod 22:25–27).
- No one would be required to work on the Sabbath (Exod 20:8–11).
- Debts would be forgiven every seven years to guard against a permanent underclass (Deut 15:1–18).
- We would cherish and protect our children from hunger and abuse (Ps 127:3–5).
- We would know that what God requires of us is "to do justice, and to love kindness, and to walk humbly" (Mic 6:8).
- We would guard our tongues, lest we say something needlessly hurtful or sordid (Mark 7:20–23).
- We would settle differences without resorting to the courts (Matt 5:21–26).
- We would have no standing army (Matt 5:34–38).
- We would value meekness instead of machismo, compassion instead of vengeance, peace instead of strife, mercy instead of retribution, poverty of spirit instead of power, and a thirst for justice instead of a lust for privilege (Matt 5:3–11).
- We would make sure that the least empowered in our society are the most honored (Matt 25:31–40).
- We would value money properly instead of worshiping it (Matt 6:24).
- We would recognize that laying down one's life for another doesn't mean killing another (John 15:13).
- We would know that all of our individual and national achievements are worth nothing if we fail to love (1 Cor 14:1–13).
- We would make no class distinctions, no gender distinctions, no I'm-better-than-you distinctions (Gal 3:28).
- We would clothe ourselves with compassion, kindness, humility, meekness, and patience (Col 3:12–13).
- We would strive for inner and outer peace by controlling our cravings (Jas 4:1–2).
- Our first allegiance would be to God, not country; much less political party (Acts 5:29).

## Christian Nation Basics

What about the handful of passages in the Hebrew Scriptures and Pauline letters, beloved by the Christian Right, that defend warfare, capital punishment, and rigid sexual mores? What are we to do with them? Is there a place for them in the Christian nation?

The way to make that determination is to discern how well such texts measure up to the Great Commandment given us by Jesus: to love at all costs, to love profligately, daringly, and sacrificially. This isn't a mushy, sentimental, feel-good sort of love, but one that desires the genuine well-being, not merely the immediate gratification, of the recipient. This kind of love is hard. But it would be the heartbeat of a Christian country, so much so that the official national motto would be "Little children, let us not love in word or talk, but in deed and in truth" (1 John 3:18).

I'd like to think this is the kind of Christian nation the Religious Right has in mind. But I'm guessing it isn't.

# Moral Distribution of Wealth

Wealth distribution in the United States is grossly skewed. According to a September 2017 Federal Reserve report, the richest 1 percent of families control nearly 40 percent of the nation's wealth. By contrast, the bottom 90 percent of families control a mere 22.8 percent.

Moreover, it's clear that the rich are getting richer and the poor poorer. The lion's share of gains from a booming stock market go to heavy investors, not the families who live from paycheck to paycheck. And those paychecks are even thinner than they were only a generation ago, when the bottom 90 percent controlled about one-third of the nation's wealth.

Christianity is not nor should be a political or economic lobby. But it does have a body of teaching about social justice and morality that's worth taking seriously, even by non-Christians. When it comes to disparity of wealth (not to mention the plutocracy it spawns), the relevant Christian principle is known as the "universal destination of goods." It states that all persons have an absolute moral right to share in the earth's resources and riches.

The argument goes something like this.

It's obvious that humans require a certain amount of material wealth both to survive and live reasonably well. This is simply an observation born from experience and ratified by reason.

Moreover, Christians and other persons of faith believe that God created the world's riches and resources to be shared fairly by all, so that everyone in fact can live reasonably well. The world's goods, in other words, are destined by God to be used and enjoyed "universally," by everyone.

Therefore, it is a moral obligation for individuals and societies to safeguard against egregious maldistribution or depletion of those riches and resources, both in the present generation and future ones.

## Moral Distribution of Wealth

The implication of the universal destination of goods principle is that the right to private property isn't absolute. In the Christian tradition, private property is a good precisely because it enables human beings to live reasonably well. But if the accumulating and hoarding of it siphons off a disproportionate share of the goods destined for all, then it becomes an evil in at least two senses: it materially robs those who live in poverty, and it spiritually corrupts those who rob them.

Saint John Paul II made this point in a particularly pithy way. There is, he argued, a "social mortgage" on all private property. "Christian tradition," he reminded us in his encyclical on work entitled *Laborem Exercens*, "has always understood the right to private property within the broader context of the right common to all to use the goods of the whole of creation. The right to private property is subordinated to the right to common use, to the fact that goods are meant for everyone." Moreover, the government, charged with protecting the common good, has a moral duty to intervene if wealth distribution becomes too disproportionate.

These are hard words for diehard capitalists and economic libertarians who believe that they have an absolute right to whatever they can accumulate, and no moral obligation to worry about the material well-being of others. But this attitude is in itself larcenous, claiming as its own what ultimately belongs to God—"the earth is the Lord's, and all that dwells therein," as the Psalmist says—and thereby diverting it from its proper universal destination.

The good news is that most of us know this. Developmental psychologists tell us that infants as young as fifteen months display a sense of fairness and even altruism. God-believers would call this a natural moral law imprinted upon conscience, while skeptics might say that it's a bit of evolutionarily selective hardware. But either way, the conclusion is that we know, deep-down, that there is indeed a universal destination of goods which we transgress at our moral peril.

# PART 5

# All Saints

# Saint of the Gutter

She was a tiny woman, and old age and hard work bent her back so that she looked even smaller. But the moral stature of Saint Teresa of Calcutta was colossal. Founder of the Missionaries of Charity, a religious order that has over six hundred facilities throughout the world, she devoted her life to serving the dying, homeless, and ill. Her hope, she often said, was to "do something beautiful for God."

Born in 1910, Teresa felt a call to the religious life at an early age and joined the Sisters of Loreto, a teaching order, when only eighteen years old. Sent to India, where she lived for the rest of her days, she spent the next two decades teaching history and geography to Indian schoolgirls. It was a tranquil, fulfilling existence.

But in September 1946, her sense of what God wanted from her abruptly changed. On a jostling, hot, and dusty train ride from Calcutta to Darjeeling, Teresa experienced what she always referred to as a "call within a call": God asked her to leave the safety of the classroom and devote herself to living with and serving the poorest of the poor.

During this revelation, Mother Teresa distinctly heard Christ's words, "I thirst." They became her spiritual reference point.

As a Christian, Teresa already believed that it was her duty to help others. But after the call within a call, she came to know, with heart as well as head, that the poor were "Christs in distressing disguises," and that just as the crucified Jesus thirsted for drink, the poor thirsted for material aid.

But "I thirst" meant something else for Teresa, too. It was an expression of burning desire for love and companionship. It signified the longing for love and comfort that Jesus felt in his final tortured moments on the cross, and the thirst for kindness, love, and compassion suffered by the world's poor.

## Part 5: All Saints

Teresa came to believe that this thirst for love was felt by everyone, rich or poor, woman or man, healthy or sickly. But she noted that it was especially pandemic among the well-off who possessed all the outward comforts of life but whose interiors were blighted by loneliness and fear.

"I thirst" is painted in the chapel, generally above the altar, of every mission founded by Teresa and her sisters, serving as a constant reminder of the order's vocation to serve the poorest of the poor with humility, gratitude, and devotion. Teresa herself, even after she'd become world famous, was always ready to pin up the ends of her blue-bordered white sari, the distinctive habit of her order, and drop to her knees to scrub toilets or bathe a leper. It's little wonder that she became known as the "saint of the gutter."

After her death in 1997, the world learned that this remarkable woman who dedicated herself to God had endured a dark night of the soul throughout the last half-century of her life. Teresa loved God and remained loyal to the call within a call, praying constantly and urging others to do likewise. But shortly after she founded the Missionaries of Charity, she found herself unable to feel the divine presence. Her letters to her confessors are heartbreaking testimonials to her forlorn sense of abandonment.

And yet she ultimately came to believe that her spiritual dryness was a divine gift that enabled her to empathize with others who likewise felt deserted by God. Shortly before she died, Teresa said that if she ever became a saint, she would be one "of darkness," forgoing the bliss of heaven to remain with and comfort those who languished in the desert searching for God.

Saints serve as exemplars of holiness for the rest of us. We learn how to be better persons by observing their lives. Teresa's great gift to us is a reminder that the entire human race thirsts, and that God calls us, as God called her, to offer one another the cool water of loving service, even when we feel low or abandoned.

Saint Teresa of Calcutta, saint of darkness, saint of the gutter, pray for us.

# Serving Christ in Friends and Strangers

She saved my life. I never actually met her, but she saved my life nonetheless. I'm confident that were it not for her, I wouldn't be a priest today, and maybe not even a Christian.

I'm talking about Dorothy Day, founder of the Catholic Workers movement.

By the time I was in my mid-twenties, I'd about given up on Christianity. So far as I could tell, American Christians were turning toward either a hyper-judgmental fundamentalism (the Moral Majority crusade had just been launched), a liberal, breezy kind of faith that tolerated everything because it believed in nothing, an arcane out-of-touch ritualism, or a safely white-bread once-a-week affair.

What I didn't see was Christianity doing much to help those who were in deep pain. The corporal works of mercy—feeding the hungry, nursing the sick, visiting the imprisoned, sheltering the homeless—were left to secular social service agencies. The corporal works of justice, prophetic action to dismantle the institutions of oppression that made works of mercy necessary in the first place, were halting and tepid.

Or so I thought. Looking back on those years now, I realize that I painted too bleak a picture. But I was young and impatient. I wanted the church to roll up its sleeves and help to make the world a better place, and it wasn't doing it quickly enough for me.

Back then, I thought my only option was to walk away from Christianity. Thankfully, a crusty, chain-smoking Jesuit, Fr. Francis Xavier Wade (of blessed memory!), sensed my turmoil and told me about Dorothy Day and the Catholic Workers.

I discovered the Christianity I'd been longing for.

## Part 5: All Saints

Dorothy, the woman who taught me how to be a Christian and thus saved my life, was born in 1897. She was a journalist and political activist before converting to Roman Catholicism. In 1933, at the height of the Great Depression, she launched the Catholic Worker movement to which she devoted the rest of her life.

Catholic Workers then and now live with the poor, the marginalized, and the hopeless. They minister to their needs, share their pain, and refrain from judging them. They establish Houses of Hospitality where street people, addicts, the mentally disturbed, and the poor can get a square meal, clothes, and a place to crash for the night. Their service is one of love and sacrifice.

Dorothy taught that when we minister to the poor, we serve Christ himself. "We see Christ and serve Christ in friends and strangers, in everyone we come in contact with," she wrote. "Christ is always with us, always asking for room in our hearts. Giving shelter or food to anyone who asks for it, or needs it, is giving it to Christ."

But Dorothy and the Catholic Workers weren't content with simply feeding and sheltering the poor. They also sought justice for them by calling out the institutional causes of poverty, neglect, prejudice, and indifference.

Day resisted and labored to convert a judicial system that unduly penalized the poor but frequently exonerated the wealthy, a government that favored big business at the expense of workers, and a military that sucked up millions of dollars that otherwise could fund much-needed improvements in infrastructure, education, and health care.

Nor did she let the church off the hook, criticizing it for too frequently bowing to Caesar by aligning with political powers and corporate principalities instead of joyfully proclaiming and generously embodying the Good News.

Dorothy believed that Christians are called to further God's kingdom by "building the new in the shell of the old." The "new" she wanted to build was actually a return to the radical hospitality and profligate love preached and practiced by the earliest Christian communities. She aimed for a society in which, as she said, it was a bit easier for humans to be good to one another.

Dorothy was no plaster saint. She could be cantankerous and impatient, and she didn't suffer fools gladly. But her vision of a Christianity that took Jesus seriously touched my soul and pulled me out of the depths. Reading her books—her memoir *The Long Loneliness* has become an American classic—and joining Catholic Workers in their works of mercy and justice were real lifesavers for me.

Thanks, Dorothy. *Ora pro nobis.*

# In Praise of Erasmus

The Protestant Reformation, whose five hundredth anniversary we recently celebrated, was launched by Martin Luther to mend a church that had grown fat and corrupt. But it also ignited a firestorm of sectarian and political warfare that blazed across Europe for the next two centuries.

Protestants fought Roman Catholics, and various Protestant sects fought each other. All disputants ardently believed that God was on their side, and this conviction too often justified horrendous atrocities.

By the time the fighting finally ceased in the mid-seventh century, an estimated ten million people had perished by sword or war-induced displacement and famine.

The Roman Catholic humanist and priest Desiderius Erasmus, born in 1466, was one of the few voices of reason in this troubled era. Erasmus was sympathetic to many of the reformers' aims. Like them, he recognized that the church needed some serious overhauling. But while many of them defended persecution as a means to achieving their ends, Erasmus pled for calm dialogue, tolerance, and a halt to the "great madness" of violence committed in the name of Christ.

It's bad enough, he argued, to draw arms for political or territorial gain. Warfare of any kind is "a monstrous pursuit" suitable only "for beasts, not men." It's "so infectious that it spreads moral corruption far and near, so unjust that it's most effectively waged by the cruelest of thieves." But to slay and maim under the pretense of defending religious faith is the worst kind of hypocrisy and cynicism. It is, insisted Erasmus, "so impious as to be utterly detestable to Christ."[1]

---

1. Sanderson Beck, "Erasmus, Anabaptists, and Mennonites," in *Guides in Peace and Justice: From Ancient Sages to the Suffragettes*, Vol. 1, 2nd ed (Santa Barbara: World Peace Communications, 2011), http://www.san.beck.org/GPJ12-Erasmus,Anabaptists.html, paras. 3, 4, .

## In Praise of Erasmus

Erasmus, born the illegitimate son of a Rotterdam priest, came by his distaste for war from two sources.

As a youth he was educated by the Brethren of the Common Life, a Roman Catholic religious community that emphasized voluntary simplicity, the cultivation of a rich interior life, and the foreswearing of violence.

After studying at the University of Paris, where he immersed himself in both classical literature and the Bible, Erasmus traveled to England and fell under the influence of the Christian humanist John Colet, who believed that the use of violence to correct social injustice and religious corruption only led to even greater evil.

The Brethren convinced Erasmus that living a genuinely Christian life meant embracing the loving-kindness preached and practiced by Jesus. This became his moral and spiritual lodestone for the rest of his life. Colet persuaded him that violence, besides being immoral, was impractical. It simply didn't work.

During his last twenty years, Erasmus became one of the most widely read authors in Europe, and he took advantage of his popularity to condemn the rise of sectarian warfare by advocating Christian nonviolence.

In his 1502 *Handbook of the Militant Christian* (the title's "militant" is synonymous with "resolute," not "martial"), Erasmus defended the claim that peace is the "highest good." Ten years later, he wrote *The Praise of Folly*, perhaps his best-known work. In it, he argued that violence, especially when committed in the name of religion, hypocritically contradicts Christ's teachings. Five years after that, in his *Education of a Christian Prince*, Erasmus urged secular rulers to so train themselves in the art of peacemaking that the science of war becomes obsolete and forgotten.

Thankfully, we American Christians are not as yet assailing one another with sword and fire. But we *are* increasingly dividing ourselves into sometimes viciously feuding camps—liberal vs. conservative, evangelical vs. progressive—whose weapons are screechy denunciations and hateful rhetoric. Moreover, just like the religious reformers in Erasmus's day, we regularly conflate partisan political allegiances with faith, which only inflames our tribal rage even more.

We could really use an Erasmus today.

# Eye to Eye

An unlettered peasant, too past his prime to work the fields any longer, intrigued his parish priest by entering the church day after day to sit silently before the tabernacle. The priest finally asked him what he was up to. Was he praying? "Not exactly," the old one replied. "I don't know many prayers. So when I come here, I just look at the good God, and He looks back at me."

This tale, usually attributed to Saint John Vianney, patron of priests, gestures at a great and somewhat startling spiritual truth: we mortals are capable of such intimacy with God that we can rest in God's presence. God becomes an immediate experience, so tangible that words and concepts are superfluous. We don't need to ponder the biology of respiration to breathe. We just breathe. Similarly, if we get to the point of simply "looking at the good God," we don't need to utter prayers or ruminate on theological questions. We just experience God, eye to eye as it were.

Many spiritual masters have recommended this kind of a relationship with God and offered advice on how to attain it. One of the wisest is Brother Lawrence of the Resurrection, a seventeenth-century lay Carmelite who called his method "practicing the presence of God."

Lawrence was a simple man whose life was outwardly unremarkable. He was probably illiterate, and certainly innocent of theology. The tasks assigned him by his superiors were all menial. He labored in his monastery's scullery for many years until arthritis lamed him, and then he worked as a cobbler. Yet before he died in 1691, pilgrims from all over Europe sought him out for spiritual counsel on how to "heart-repose" in the Lord.

Lawrence was inspired by Saint Paul's recommendation to pray without ceasing, but also initially perplexed by it. How is such a thing possible? We humans engage in everyday tasks and occasional emergencies that demand our full attention. We also sleep each night. So how can prayer be ceaseless?

The trick, Lawrence discovered, is to pray with an intentionally short mantra ("My God, I am yours," for example, or "Lord, fashion me." I prefer the Orthodox Jesus Prayer: "Lord Jesus Christ, son of the living God, have mercy on me") that "keeps the mind fastened on God alone." The mantra is repeated, attuned to the rhythm of breathing, until it becomes such a part of who we are that we utter it silently, in our depths, regardless of whether we're awake or asleep. It weaves into the fabric of our existence, sinking from our lips to our hearts to make "the time of prayer no different than any other time."

The mantra isn't a magical incantation, nor is practicing the presence of God an auto-hypnotic method of reducing psychological anxiety or tension. Instead, Brother Lawrence's method aims at calming the spirit and focusing the mind so that we're ever alert to the always-present God.

Then, whatever we do, whether commonplace or extraordinary, is done in God's company. We cobble shoes, and God sits beside us. We prepare food, and God is there. We drive to work, surf the internet, bathe our children, clean house, shop for groceries, write books, govern nations, mourn losses, take a nap: in all of these activities, we pray ceaselessly in a "wordless and secret conversation" with God. We look at the good God, and God looks back at us.

When we've broken through to this heart-repose in the presence of God, we discover something wonderful: our more conventional ways of praying are vitalized. Extemporaneous prayers that in the past focused too often on our own desires and needs—"God, help me!" "God, fix this!" "God, grant me that!"—become expressions of profound awe and deep gratitude. Formal liturgical prayers that may have been muted by familiarity transfigure into heartfelt hymns of praise to the Lord.

Theologian Karl Rahner predicted a generation ago that "the devout Christian of the future will either be a mystic, one who has experienced something, or he will cease to be anything at all." The old peasant who lovingly sat eye to eye with God, as well as simple Brother Lawrence at his cobbler's bench, would've understood what Rahner had in mind.

# The Grand Experiment

In 1845, Henry David Thoreau, then in his late twenties, borrowed an ax, went to the woods surrounding the Massachusetts village of Concord, and began felling trees. He used the timber to build the small cabin he lived in for two years, two months, and two days. His book *Walden*, a journal of his discoveries during those twenty-six months, is a genuine American classic. Although Thoreau wasn't a Christian, his paean to the simple life has much to teach us Christians.

Thoreau didn't go to the woods because he was a misanthrope who despised the company of others. Nor, not being a particularly religious man, did he go there to commune with God. (On his deathbed, when someone urged him to make peace with his Maker, Thoreau quipped that he wasn't aware of ever having quarreled with him.)

Instead, Thoreau conducted an experiment, the grandest one imaginable. "I went to the woods because I wished to live deliberately, to front only the essential facts of life, and see if I could not learn what it had to teach, and not, when I came to die, discover that I had not lived." He wanted, he wrote, to "live deeply" and "suck the marrow of life."[1]

In a consumerist culture like ours that valorizes worldly success, the good life is primarily measured in terms of wealth and power. Sucking the marrow of life means having enough money to buy anything we could possibly crave. But for Thoreau, it meant living "deliberately," or mindfully, to discern what we should want out of life.

Thoreau observed that his friends and acquaintances in Concord seemed fixated on accumulating as much land, property, and wealth as they could. Accordingly, they pushed themselves to labor ever more

---

1. Henry David Thoreau, *Walden and Civil Disobedience* (New York: Signet, 2012), 32.

backbreakingly to earn money so they could buy more things. But the tragedy, as Thoreau saw it, was that more was never enough for them. Each new acquisition only reignited new appetites, until they found themselves in what the twentieth-century economist John Kenneth Galbraith called the trap of the squirrel or hamster wheel: running faster and faster in pursuit of higher incomes and more consumer goods, but getting no closer to the genuinely good life.

The nascent consumer frenzy that troubled Thoreau in his century is full blown in ours. Commodity addiction—what some commentators wittily but aptly call "affluenza"—is out of control. We shop when we're happy, when we're depressed, or when we're just bored. We purchase goods, mostly on credit, in hundreds of thousands of actual and virtual stores. We just can't get our fill of stuff—not surprisingly, since we define ourselves and others by what we own. The way out, fortunately, isn't rocket science, but it does call for self-discipline. According to Thoreau, the trick is: "Simplify, simplify, simplify!"

What's called for is purging the mania for accumulation that clutters our souls with inordinate desires and our garages with junk we jubilantly buy but quickly tire of. Simplifying our inner and outer worlds revitalizes our jaded spiritual palates, enabling us to relish life's enriching marrow instead of gorging ourselves on junk food substitutes.

When we discipline our desires and simplify our day-to-day living, we make space for a rediscovery of the wonder at the world we had as kids. We retrieve the ability for grateful astonishment that the consumer culture stole from us.

We are once again able to be attentive to and appreciative of the everyday but quite extraordinary gifts that the world offers: the beauty of a lark's song, the delicacy of a dandelion gone to seed, the stateliness of a heron, and the tenderness of a lover's smile.

We remember that it's more important to be than to have, to let go than to clutch, to be happy instead of settling for a fleeting satiation. This is what it means to "front the essential facts of life." This is how, as Thoreau wrote, we open "the channel of purity."

To discover as we lie dying that we never really lived, the fate that Thoreau dreaded, is a terrible thing. When the time comes for us to return to our ancestors, we should be able to leave the earth with profound gratitude for the life we led. Getting stuck on the squirrel wheel won't get us there,

## Part 5: All Saints

regardless of how frenetically we run. We're better off going to the woods now and then listening, as Thoreau did, to what the trees have to tell us.

# A Lesson from the Gulag

He grew up in a rough-and-tumble Pennsylvania coal town, and he learned at an early age to use his fists. He got into so many brawls that his exasperated father once frog-marched him to the town's police station and demanded that his headstrong son be sent to reform school. (He wasn't.)

But the boy, whose name was Walter Ciszek, underwent a sea change when he was thirteen. He decided to take Holy Orders, and thereafter the energy he'd poured into street fighting was redirected to academic study and spiritual formation, culminating in his 1937 ordination as a Jesuit priest.

Because he'd grown up in an ethnic Polish family, Ciszek was fluent in the tongue of his ancestors, and he perfected his Russian while in seminary. His dream was to become an underground priest in the officially atheist Soviet Union, and he got his chance when the chaos of World War II erupted. Sneaking across the USSR's border in 1940, he posed as a laborer while covertly ministering to fellow workers.

But secrets are hard to keep in a totalitarian state. Inevitably, word leaked out that Ciszek was a priest. He was arrested, charged with espionage, held for five years in solitary confinement, convicted, and then shipped off to a Siberian hard labor gulag.

Attorney General Robert Kennedy negotiated a 1963 deal with the USSR to repatriate the by then 58-year-old Ciszek. Once back on US soil, he wrote two books about his experiences. The first, *With God in Russia*, is a gripping memoir of his struggle to survive in the gulag. His second book, *He Leadeth Me*, centered on an insight into the meaning of divine will that came to Ciszek during his long imprisonment.

Prior to his years of captivity, Ciszek, like many of us, persistently confused his self-assertion with God's will, immediately assuming that whatever he wanted for himself—ordination, membership in the Jesuits, the covert mission to the Soviet Union—God wanted as well. But because imprisonment scuttled Ciszek's plans and dreams, he concluded that he must have gotten things terribly wrong. After all, why would God have permitted him to be thrown into prison if what God willed for him was identical to what Ciszek willed for himself?

This realization thrust Ciszek into a dark night of despair in which, he writes, he lost for a time the "last shreds" of his faith. But the darkness lifted and faith returned once it dawned on him what divine will actually is.

People typically think that God's will for them points to a specific assignment. God wants a candidate to win an elective office; God wants a teenager to score the winning touchdown; God wants me to write this book. This way of thinking implies that each of us has a divinely prearranged destiny, and that we let God down if we fail to reach it.

But Ciszek discovered that what God wills for us isn't necessarily this or that specific goal. God's will is more about the here-and-now than the future. "The plain and simple truth is that God's will is what he actually wills to send us each day, in the way of circumstances, places, people, and problems."

What Ciszek means is that God doesn't micromanage our lives by preordaining who we'll be or what projects we'll undertake. To do so would rob us of freedom. Instead, God's will for us is more about how to do than what to do, although the two are obviously related. We're called to be fully present to whatever situation we happen to be in, mindfully responsive to "circumstances, places, people, and problems" in ways worthy of creatures made in the likeness of a loving God. Wherever we find ourselves, be it prison, classroom, factory, unhappy marriage, illness, or professional failure, God wants us to be charitable, compassionate, humble, just, reverent, hopeful, and patient.

God's will isn't that we be spared from failure or disappointment—nowhere are we promised a trouble-free existence—but that we refuse to allow the hard times, when they come, to make us less than what, by God's grace, we are. This is the lesson Walter Ciszek learned in the gulag, and it liberated his spirit. If we take it to heart, it will free us as well.

# He Got Christ Out of the Churches

Hanging on the wall of my library is an item I cherish: a framed 1926 telegram acknowledging a donation to the Winter Distress League, a London-based relief organization that collected coal, clothes, and food for unemployed workers and their families. It's signed by one G. A. Studdert Kennedy, Woodbine Willie.

Born June 27, 1883, Geoffrey Anketell "Woodbine Willie" Studdert Kennedy was one of the hundreds of padres who served in the British army during World War I. He saw action on the Somme, at Messines Ridge, and in the final Western offensive, was awarded the Military Cross for conspicuous bravery, and was celebrated by the Ministry of War as a national hero.

But then, to the Ministry's shock and chagrin, Studdert Kennedy became the most ardent Christian pacifist of his generation. His nightmarish experiences in the war had knocked all the patriotic jingoism and romantic illusions about armed conflict out of him. "There are no words," he wrote, "foul and filthy enough to describe war."

He knew what he was talking about. Many committed pacifists before and since Studdert Kennedy's time have never experienced combat. He did, and its horror changed him.

Ordained in 1910 in the Church of England, Studdert Kennedy spent the years before the war as a slum priest ministering to wretchedly impoverished parishes. Wishing to share the poverty of his flock, he deliberately served parishes with the smallest income, driving his good wife to distraction by giving away money and household items—including, once, even their mattress.

Afire like most of his countrymen with war fever when the Great War erupted, Studdert Kennedy enthusiastically enlisted in the British Army in 1916. Battlefield padres were generally despised by soldiers as unctuous do-gooders who stayed safely behind the lines. But they quickly came to admire Studdert Kennedy, affectionately calling him "Woodbine Willie" after the brand of cigarettes he regularly handed out to them, because he didn't hesitate to risk his life to rescue and offer spiritual solace to the wounded.

The nickname stuck with him for the rest of his days.

As the horrendous war that eventually took seventeen million lives and shattered Europe dragged on, Studdert Kennedy grew convinced that the evils of economic injustice he'd witnessed and struggled against as a civilian priest were matched by the wickedness of war. His change of heart became total in June 1917 when his personal aide, a youth of nineteen years, was killed. Studdert Kennedy found him "leaning against a heap of sandbags, his head in his hands, and a great hole in his back."[1] He buried the boy with his own hands in a bomb crater.

After the war, Woodbine Willie used his status as a national hero to speak and write ceaselessly against war and economic inequality. He outraged both political and ecclesial powerbrokers, but thousands of war-damaged veterans and tens of thousands of people who lived in dire poverty loved the small-statured, floppy-eared, sad-eyed, and golden-tongued padre who spoke up for them.

In over twenty volumes of prose and verse, as well as hundreds of speeches and sermons, Studdert Kennedy urged Christians to take Jesus's message of peace, compassion, and justice seriously. The problem, he said, was that the church preferred a domesticated, nonthreatening Jesus, safely tucked away "amid the lilies of the altar, with the sweet incense of worship rising round Him, a weekly refuge from a distraught and vulgar world." But, he warned, "You cannot keep Christ in your churches; he will break them into pieces if you try." Churchmen, he said, might shy away from the messy business of rolling up their sleeves and doing something about poverty and violence. Christ wouldn't.[2]

When Studdert Kennedy died in 1929, utterly worn out by his post-war crusade to get Christ out of the churches and into the streets, hospitals, and slums, thousands of grateful veterans and workers lined the route of his funeral entourage. As the hearse bearing his coffin passed by, they lovingly tossed packets of Woodbines onto it.

---

1. G. A. Studdert Kennedy, "Burying the Dead," in *After War, Is Faith Possible?*, ed. Kerry Walters, 44–45 (Eugene, OR: Cascade, 2008), 44.

2. G. A. Studdert Kennedy, "Getting Christ Out of the Churches," in *After War, Is Faith Possible?*, ed. Kerry Walters, 175–76 (Eugene, OR: Cascade, 2008), 175.

# Oxford's Inklings

Had I lived in Oxford during the thirties and forties, I know exactly where I would've eaten my lunch on Tuesdays: the Eagle and Child pub, affectionately called the Bird and Baby by the locals.

It was there and then that some of the twentieth century's most creative English-speaking Christians met to chat about ideas and books. They called themselves the Inklings, partly because they were all writers with inevitably ink-stained fingers, but also because they wanted to convey in their novels and verse hints or inklings of God's existence.

I'd have loved to eavesdrop on their conversations.

The Inklings were pulled together by C. S. Lewis in late 1933. He and J. R. R. Tolkien, both Oxford University professors, along with editor and author Charles Williams, would become the group's three best known members. But all of the dozen or so writers who made up the group were remarkable.

Lewis organized the Inklings because he felt the need, even in the early 1930s, for an alternative to Oxford's increasingly secular and anti-Christian ethos. Then as now, academics who were committed Christians were often lonely outliers at universities and colleges, held at arm's length by disdainful colleagues. Lewis was so grateful for the boon companionship of the Inklings that he dedicated one of his books to them.

In addition to their Tuesdays at the Bird and Baby, the Inklings also met on Thursday nights in Lewis's college rooms.

At the Thursday gatherings, manuscripts which individual Inklings were working on were read and discussed. Tolkien shared *The Hobbit* (which Lewis initially didn't think much of) as well as pieces of his *Lord of the Rings* trilogy. Lewis offered the group portions of his Narnia stories (which Tolkien never warmed up to), as well as his space trilogy. Charles Williams, an editor at Oxford University Press and Dante scholar, read selections from his own novels-in-progress, especially *Descent into Hell* and *All Hallows' Eve*.

The Tuesday get-togethers at the Bird and Baby were more informal, but by all accounts the conversation was still scintillating. The Inklings were incurably impatient of small talk. Their conversations at the pub, lubricated with pints of good English ale, revolved around literature, theology, and faith.

What drew the Inklings together was their shared conviction that the world is aglow with the presence of God, a reality repudiated by science and eclipsed by the hustle and bustle of everyday life. They worried that a disenchanted world is soul-killing. As the French filmmaker Robert Bresson once said, life under such circumstances becomes one-dimensionally stupid and boring.

The Inklings were hopeful that fiction and verse could be vehicles for reawakening us to the reality of God. Lewis spoke for them all when he said, "in life and art both, we are always trying to catch in our net of successive moments something that is not successive." He knew it was increasingly difficult for people today to be awakened to the "not successive" dimension of reality, but he was confident that "it is sometimes done—or very, very nearly done—in stories."

Tolkien heartily agreed. In his landmark essay "On Fairy Stories," he argued that myths and fantasy narratives appeal to us because we glimpse in them something for which we yearn: a vision of reality that infuses deep meaning into the everyday world and elicits wonder, delight, and gratitude. The Christian Gospels, Tolkien noted, are able to do this. They have the same revivifying function, in other words, as myths and fairy stories. The saving difference is that they're also true.

It's no surprise, given what the Inklings hoped to accomplish, that their fiction and verse were largely allegorical (even though Tolkien had some reservations about the genre; in unskilled hands, he believed, it could become tediously didactic). Aslan in Lewis's *Narnia* books is a Christ-figure, Tolkien's *Lord of the Rings* an epic of salvific self-sacrifice (what he called "eucatastrophe," joy arising from despair), and Charles Williams's beautifully strange novels focus on the cosmic struggle between God and dark powers and principalities.

Tolkien's, Lewis's, and Williams's imaginative retelling of the Christian story succeeded in re-enchanting the world for millions of readers. No Inkling could have guessed that those Tuesday and Thursday meetings, crackling with genius, laughter, and good will, would have such a colossal impact on so many.

It's almost the stuff of fairy stories.

# The Dumb Ox

He was the classic schoolboy nerd. Had he lived in the twenty-first instead of the thirteenth century, he'd probably have sported a pencil-stuffed pocket protector. He was pudgy, shy, physically awkward, and so slow of speech that his classmates called him the "dumb ox." (Cruelty among schoolboys unfortunately traverses time and place.)

Yet his teacher, Albertus Magnus, one of the greatest philosophers of the day, saw genius in young Tomasso d'Aquino. He predicted that when this dumb ox found his tongue, his words would ring throughout the world.

Albertus was right. The boy, better known as Thomas Aquinas, the Latinized version of his name, became a Christian theologian whose writings remain important even now, seven centuries later. Although Rome initially condemned some of them, he was eventually rehabilitated and canonized.

In 1244, while still a teenager, Thomas joined the Dominicans, a newly-launched religious order dedicated to preaching, teaching, and scholarship. He trained and subsequently taught at the best universities Europe had to offer. His intellect was astounding. He absorbed everything he read, and his mental dexterity and powers of concentration enabled him to dictate two or more works simultaneously to different scribes.

The dumb ox was also tireless. Although he died at the age of forty-nine, his writings on theology, philosophy, politics, morality, and Scripture fill dozens of volumes.

Brainy though he was, Thomas was first and foremost a person of deep faith. His rich spirituality not only fueled his theological and philosophical reflections, but also found expression in a handful of beautiful hymns. Perhaps his best known is *Pange Lingua*:

> Sing, my tongue, the Savior's glory,

# The Dumb Ox

> Of his Flesh the mystery sing;
> Of the blood, all price exceeding,
> Shed by our immortal King,
> Destined from the world's redemption,
> From a noble womb to spring.

The task of theology is to express the truths of the faith in ways that acknowledge and address the concerns and perspectives of each generation. This requires having a good handle on the latest advances in learning as well as a profound appreciation of what's essential and what's peripheral to the faith. The best theologians think rigorously and systematically about God, but communicate their insights in understandable ways that deepen the ordinary Christian's comprehension of and devotion to the faith.

Thomas had both of these qualities down pat.

The new learning of his day revolved around the ancient philosopher Aristotle, whose works were only then being rediscovered by the West. Thomas immediately saw that the rational analysis and empirical method defended by Aristotle could invigorate Christian theology.

In several of his books, most notably his masterpiece *Summa Theologiae*, he offered a theological vision which synthesized Aristotelian philosophy and Christian revelation. Following Aristotle, Thomas argued that rational scrutiny of the material world tells us that God, the necessary First Cause of all that is, exists. Reason also sheds a good deal of light on questions involving ethics and psychology.

But scriptural revelation and tradition are equally important, disclosing as they do Christian truths, such as the doctrine of the Trinity, that unaided reason can neither discover nor entirely fathom. In Thomas's view, there is no conflict between faith and reason. Truth is one, can never contradict itself, and always leads to God.

Some of Thomas's writing is highly technical. But he also wrote more-or-less popular works (the aforementioned *Summa Theologiae* is actually one of them) that are perfectly comprehensible to nonspecialists willing to do some serious study. Even today, with just a bit of patience and discipline, readers can study him profitably—and pleasurably, too. Anyone wishing to give Thomas a try might begin with a section of his *Summa* known as the "Treatise on Virtues."

The best theologians are humble, knowing that their efforts to speak about God inevitably fall short. How can finite minds, even the very brightest, hope to do more than gesture at the Divine Mystery?

## Part 5: All Saints

And so it was that a few months before his death in 1274, Thomas had a mystical vision of God while celebrating Mass that caused him to cease work, almost in mid-sentence, on his *Summa*. "Compared with what I have seen," he said afterwards, "all that I have written is but straw."

Yet the dumb ox's straw continues to nourish us even today.

# A Sacrosanct Right

She told friends that her status as a Roman Catholic nun would protect her, despite the many death threats she had received.

She was mistaken.

Two decades ago, while on her way to a community meeting in a town on the edge of the Brazilian rainforest, Sister Dorothy Stang was confronted by two men. Bizarrely, they asked the diminutive seventy-four-year-old if she was carrying weapons.

She responded that God's word was the only weapon she needed. When she pulled out her Bible and read "Blessed are the poor in spirit" to the two men, they shot her. Then they pumped five more bullets into her as she lay face down in the dirt.

The murder of Sister Dorothy shocked and saddened the thousands of Brazilian campesinos or peasants she had championed for three decades. Inspired by a faith which teaches that service to the poor, sick, homeless, imprisoned, and hungry is service to Christ himself, she had dedicated herself to advocating for Brazil's marginalized peasants and the rainforest in which they lived against unscrupulous entrepreneurs who cared for nothing but profit and power.

Born into a large Roman Catholic family in Dayton, Ohio, Stang joined the Sisters of Notre Dame de Namur, an order dedicated to aiding poor people, especially women and children, in the world's most abandoned places. In 1966, ten years after taking her final vows, she was sent to Brazil to do precisely that.

Sister Dorothy quickly fell in love with her exotic new home, becoming fluent in Portuguese and eventually requesting Brazilian citizenship. Initially, her work consisted of the standard missionary duties of nuns: teaching children and helping overworked priests serve their extended parishes. But as she became increasingly familiar with the grinding poverty endured by the campesinos, her ministry changed. She came to believe that God was calling her to do more than offer peasants charity, important as that was. She was to bring them justice as well.

Brazilian peasants, who scratched out a precarious existence on small farms in and around the rainforest, were being driven off their plots by ranching and timber conglomerates that slashed and burned their way through the forest. A few immensely wealthy ranchers—nearly 50 percent of Brazil's arable land is in the hands of just a few families—wanted more and more rainforest cleared to graze beef or grow grain to feed cattle. The barons wanted to harvest the millions of feet of straight and true lumber growing in the forest.

Between them, they formed an unholy partnership that mercilessly gouged the peasants and mindlessly destroyed the rainforest. Sister Dorothy saw that defending poor sharecroppers and subsistence farmers also meant advocating for the forest that surrounded and sustained them.

The campesinos, Stang insisted, "have the sacrosanct right to aspire to a better life on land where they can live and work with dignity while respecting the environment." This is a right possessed by all humans by virtue of their being children of God. It is inviolable—"sacrosanct"—and to deprive anyone of it is an affront against God.

Moreover, the "death of the forest," proclaimed Stang, "is the end of our life," not just because its devastation means the ruin of small farmers, but also because the rainforest is one of the world's natural wonders. Its wanton exploitation for commercial gain—to date, about 20 percent of its 1.6 million acres has been destroyed—is an assault on the beauty and grandeur of God's earth that leads to both material and spiritual impoverishment.

Stang's murder—contracted, it turned out, by rich landowners—galvanized worldwide resistance to the timber and ranching oligarchs exploiting the Brazilian peasantry and rainforest. Those gunshots at the edge of the forest ended her life, but not her ministry.

Sister Dorothy's crusade for the sacrosanct right of a decent, planet-friendly life invites all of us, especially those who believe in God, to consider what we owe our fellow humans and the planet we call home. Do we construct walls or bridges? Welcome or rebuff the needy? Build pipelines or green energy technologies? Labor for justice or oligarchy?

In a word, do we serve God or Mammon?

# PART 6

# Behold the Beauty

# Gauguin's Questions

By all accounts, the post-expressionist painter Paul Gauguin was a pretty unpleasant guy. He abandoned his wife and children, kept company with prostitutes (from whom he contracted the syphilis that finally killed him in 1903), quarreled with fellow artists when he wasn't mooching off them, and bullied poor Vincent van Gogh into a nervous breakdown.

Among his many unsavory habits was foot-dragging when it came to honoring his debts. So Gauguin periodically fled Europe to escape pesky creditors. His preferred sanctuaries were South Pacific islands, particularly Tahiti, and they inspired some of his finest canvases. Blemished though his character may've been, Gauguin was a superb artist.

The work that's widely recognized as his masterpiece is in the Boston Museum of Fine Arts. It's a large canvas, more than twelve feet in length, which Gauguin completed in 1897 while living in Tahiti.

In the upper left corner of the painting, Gauguin scrawled three questions, curiously omitting their question marks: *D'où venons nous, Que sommes nous, Où allons nous*: "Where do we come from? What are we? Where are we going?" Then, moving from the right side of the canvas to the left, he painted images that allude to his three questions: a newborn infant, an adult with upward stretching hands, as if asking heaven a question, and an old and fragile woman.

The beauty of this painting, rich with shades of blue, violet, and gold, takes one's breath away. But so do the questions Gauguin asks, because they're the most fundamental ones that we humans can pose. They're so foundational, in fact, that our lives are the poorer if we never ask them.

Gauguin knew what we know: we're the only creatures on earth capable of wondering about our origin (birth), our destination (death), and what happens in between (life). When we ask his three questions, our intent isn't to calculate actuarial probabilities or map the biology of *Homo sapiens*. We're asking whether or not human life is meaningful.

Some philosophers maintain that the question is nonsensical. Meaning, they say, is a property of sentences. We can ask if the sentence "Life is meaningful" is meaningful, but we can't ask the same of life itself. To do so is to fall into a category mistake, a confusion of apples and oranges, much like asking whether your pet goldfish has mastered calculus or whether my toothbrush needs glasses. It's to take gibberish seriously.

But the philosophers are mistaken, because we know perfectly well what we mean when we ask about the meaning of life, and it's far from nonsensical. We want to know whether we're mere evolutionary byproducts or beings whose lives are somehow intrinsically purposeful and worth living. Are our births, lives, and deaths mere random occurrences, or do they gesture at a larger, comprehensive design?

One possible answer is that we construct our own meaning through the life choices and relationships we make. Another is that the cruelty and arbitrariness of life gives the lie to any meaningful design. We struggle as best we can through an absurd life and then we die. A third possibility is that there's a deep meaning to our lives because they and everything else in the universe are the creations of a loving, wise, and providential God.

Some questions can be answered pretty definitively. Gauguin's can't. When it comes to fundamental questions about our existence, we simply have to use what evidence we've found as a springboard for a leap of faith. We plunk down our money and take what we get. This unavoidable uncertainty might lead some into thinking that it's foolish to even bother asking for the who, what, and where of life.

But it's important to know this: the very fact that we ask such questions indicates something profoundly important about us. It suggests that we're never satisfied with the prosaic here-and-now, but are innately and restlessly curious about who we are and how we fit into the universe. And because nature, as Aristotle said, abhors a vacuum, the very presence of such an itch suggests that there's something in reality capable of scratching it.

Sometimes, in other words, the questions we ask are also the answers we seek. Perhaps that's why Gauguin omitted the question marks.

# The Sistine Gem

In a 1509 poem that combined humor and seriousness, Michelangelo lamented that his work on the Sistine Chapel ceiling was doing a number on his body.

"I've already grown a goiter from this torture, hunched up here like a cat," he wrote. "My stomach's squashed under my chin, my beard's pointing at heaven, my brain's crushed in a casket, my breast twists like a harpy's. My brush, above me all the time, dribbles paint so my face makes a fine floor for droppings!"

The complaint ended with the astonishing confession that "I'm not in the right place; I'm no painter!"—astonishing, because by anyone's estimation, Michelangelo's frescoes in the Sistine Chapel are works of sheer genius.

The famous ceiling of the Sistine Chapel, the creation of which dribbled paint onto Michelangelo's upturned face for four long years, was publicly unveiled on All Saints' Day in 1512. The project had been commissioned by Pope Julius II, an unsavory character who bribed his way onto Peter's Throne, but who turned out to be a generous patron of the arts.

Michelangelo, who always considered himself first and foremost a sculptor, was busily at work on the extravagant tomb Julius had ordered for his postmortem repose when the pontiff asked him to take on the Sistine job. Michelangelo demurred; he'd never worked with fresco. But Julius insisted, so the sculptor laid down his chisel and picked up a brush.

The Sistine Chapel, which takes its name from Sixtus IV, the pope who had it built in the 1470s, is architecturally unremarkable except for its dimensions: 132 feet long, forty-four feet wide, and sixty-eight feet high, reckoned by Sixtus to be the same as Solomon's Temple in Jerusalem. There are six upper-tiered windows on the facing long walls. The lower tiers boast paintings by Renaissance masters like Botticelli and Raphael.

## Part 6: Behold the Beauty

At the time Michelangelo began work on it, the chapel's barrel-shaped ceiling was unimaginatively painted to resemble a starry sky. Julius wanted a complete makeover, something to quicken the heart and enliven the spirit. That's exactly what Michelangelo gave him.

Michelangelo's ceiling heralds the coming of Christ without ever explicitly depicting him. Running down its center are nine scenes from the Old Testament, starting with the Creation and ending with the immediate aftermath of the Noahic Flood. The best-known panel, reproduced in thousands of prints and posters, is Michelangelo's dramatic vision of the creation of humans, with God and Adam yearningly stretching toward each other.

In each of the ceiling's four corners, Michelangelo painted additional Old Testament scenes such as David's slaying of Goliath and Moses holding aloft the bronze serpent. He framed all four sides with portraits of the Hebrew prophets who foretold the coming of the Messiah, and of Greco-Roman sibyls, female soothsayers from the classical world.

There's nothing delicate about Michelangelo's portraits. If that's the kind of painting you're looking for, his fellow artist Raphael is your man. Michelangelo's figures—Moses, Noah, Adam, the sibyls, God—are majestic titans with rippling muscles, flowing robes, and taut facial expressions. Michelangelo the sculptor said he painted them as if he were chiseling three-dimensional figures. The rich colors he used, happily restored to their original intensity by late twentieth-century cleanings, are stunning.

Ever the perfectionist, Michelangelo refused to let anyone, even Pope Julius, see his work until it was finished. The pope, unaccustomed to being refused anything, grew so exasperated that he once actually struck Michelangelo several blows. Finally unwilling to tolerate any more delays, he angrily threatened to have Michelangelo "thrown from the top of your scaffolding!"

Realizing he'd pushed the pontiff's patience to the breaking point, Michelangelo at last threw the chapel doors open. Vasari, whose 1550 *Lives of the Artists* is an entertaining compendium of gossip about the era's painters and sculptors, wrote that "when the work was uncovered, everyone rushed to see it and were dumbfounded with admiration." Coming from the frequently snarky Vasari, this was high praise indeed.

Michelangelo finished the ceiling frescoes when he was in his midthirties. Thirteen years later, he returned to the chapel to paint the Last

Judgment on the altar wall. This second fresco is magnificent. It's the final facet in the Sistine Chapel gem carved by the sculptor Michelangelo.

Not too shabby for a guy who never thought of himself as a genuine painter.

# Like Anemones

Sometimes spiritual truths are better expressed through metaphor, analogy, and poetry than straightforward theology or learned biblical commentary.

Consider, for example, the anemone.

As gardeners everywhere know, the anemone is a gorgeous flower that closes its petals in the dark hours of night and reopens them at dawn, slowly, until they're splayed wide to absorb as much sunlight as possible.

We admire and even revel in the anemone's colorful beauty. But as the Bohemian-Austrian poet Rainer Maria Rilke noted in one of his "Sonnets to Orpheus," the flower's unfolding also offers us a powerful image of spiritual fruition.

The anemone, he writes, has a "muscle of infinite reception" that opens bit by bit "until into her lap the polyphonic / light of the loud skies pours down." So wide do her petals open, and so saturated with the sun does she become, that when dusk falls the flower is loath to close again.[1]

When, Rilke asks, will we humans become, like the anemone, "at last open and receivers"? When will we dare to throw wide the petals of our hearts and allow ourselves to be saturated by God? That we don't is perplexing, given that this is what each of us actually longs for at our deepest core.

A good part of the explanation for why we don't imitate the anemone is that we often misunderstand the foundational desire for God with which we're imprinted, and thereby settle for less than what we really yearn for.

What we want from life is a deep and abiding sense of purpose, the security of permanence, and the fulfillment of love. These human desires

---

1. Ranier Maria Rilke, *Sonnets to Orpheus*, trans. Edward Snow (New York: North Point, 2005), 69.

are designed both to enrich our lives and draw us ever closer to what can ultimately satisfy them: God.

But we get easily distracted by more immediate-to-hand substitutes. Instead of mindfully searching for what genuinely nourishes us, we settle for fast food. Some of us devour money, and others, prestige. Still others gobble up power or knowledge or thrills. A frightening number of us binge regularly on soul-numbing and heart-sclerotic modes of entertainment served up on smartphones or big screen televisions.

We open ourselves just wide enough to grab these less-than-satisfying objects of desire—objects which, truth to tell, are more destructive than not—and once we have them, we snap shut again, fearful that they might slip away if we don't clutch them with all our strength.

Allowing ourselves to be diverted from the true object of our desire is to fall into what Henry David Thoreau once called a life of quiet desperation. Money, prestige, power, thrills, and shallow entertainment satisfy us for a while, perhaps, but can't in any way give us the deep meaning and purpose we really crave. There's always a restlessness, a nagging and usually unnamed discontent, that haunts us.

As Augustine noted sixteen centuries ago, our hearts are restless until they rest in God.

Even worse, in our closed-in blindness, we too often scurry to sooth our underlying disquiet by piling up even more of the very fast food menu items that triggered it in the first place. And so we become trapped, like hamsters on wheels running frenetically in place faster and faster under the delusion that we're actually getting somewhere.

As Rilke pointed out, the anemone offers the example of a better way. Instead of clutching our fast food substitutes so tightly (and desperately) that the petals of our hearts clamp shut, we need to open them to God. We need to become, as Rilke recommends, receivers.

Doing so loosens our grip and flings away the things with which we've stiffened our spirits. This in turn leaves plenty of room for our own "muscle of infinite reception"—the soul—to stretch wide for God, the Source and Fulfillment of all our desires.

Of course, our capacity for God isn't literally infinite. That's a bit of poetic license on Rilke's part. Just as the anemone, for all its stretching, can never contain the immensity of the sun, so the unfolding of our hearts can never clear an open space large enough to contain the infinite and eternal God.

Part 6: Behold the Beauty

But if we expand our hearts we can be suffused with God, just as the wide-open anemone can be saturated with sunlight. And that's plenty good enough.

# Hidden in Plain Sight

It's a rare visitor to Amsterdam who resists the temptation to stroll through the city's famous red light district.

The boundaries of the district are clearly demarcated by—what else?—actual red lights set into the cobbled streets. The main corridor, typically filled with slightly embarrassed tourists and snickering teenage boys, boasts strip joints, cannabis bars, and storefronts flamboyantly displaying a bewildering array of sex paraphernalia. On the side streets, scantily clad women sit, stand, or woodenly gyrate behind full-length plate glass windows, advertising what they hope to sell.

All in all, Amsterdam's red light district comes off as a rather sad and tawdry place.

Nestled within it, though, like a gem in a barnyard muck heap, is something precious. It takes some effort to locate. But as the Dutch philosopher Spinoza wrote, all good things are as difficult as they are rare.

I'm referring to the exquisite chapel hidden away in the top three stories of a seventeenth-century house on the *Oudezijds Voorburgwal* canal. It's known as *Ons' Lieve Heer op Solder*, "Our Dear Lord in the Attic."

From the outside, the gabled building that holds the chapel looks like just any other tall and narrow canal house. That was the whole point, because it was meant to hide the worship space of an outlawed religion. In 1578, Protestant Amsterdam forbade Roman Catholics from public celebrations of their faith. Private gatherings, on the other hand, were tolerated.

The canal house dates back to 1630. Three decades later, Jan Hartman, a Roman Catholic German merchant who settled in Amsterdam, bought it and began transforming its upper floors into a secret church where he and his co-religionists could gather for Mass.

Entering through the front door like neighbors coming to call, worshipers climbed an extremely steep and narrow staircase to get to the

## Part 6: Behold the Beauty

main sanctuary. Its beauty is absolutely breathtaking. The nave, with long balconies on either side, culminates in a magnificent chancel containing a marble altar, columns, and a Rubenesque painting of the baptism of Jesus. The whole space is laid out so cunningly that it feels much larger than it actually is. And because the chapel is above street level noise, a tranquil silence pervades it.

Standing in the chapel, you can feel the centuries of prayer offered up in it. You can sense the presence of God. It's a holy place, hidden in plain sight.

*Ons' Lieve Heer op Solder* is a reminder of one of the most basic truths of faith: God "plays in ten thousand places," as poet Gerard Manley Hopkins noted, no matter how ordinary or commonplace they are. But for one reason or other, we often fail to discern the sacred presence. God remains hidden in plain sight.

Sometimes God remains hidden in plain sight because, not expecting him in the quotidian, we look for him to amaze us with flashy, Hollywood-sized pyrotechnics. At other times, we get so sidetracked by the sheer busyness of everyday life that it's hard for us to see beyond the immediate task at hand. Consuming ambition or bewitchment by our hedonistic culture may also blind us to the ubiquity of the divine presence.

Sadly, God may also be hidden in plain sight within houses of worship. We can become so focused on externalities—committee work, stewardship drives, physical upkeep, and congregational building—that our churches and temples become, as the nineteenth-century philosopher Friedrich Nietzsche mordantly said, the whited sepulchers of God rather than sacred spaces.

Thankfully, however, the God whom our spiritual myopia sometimes keeps hidden in plain sight perpetually breaks through. He reveals himself in the face of a laughing child and the courage of a refugee. God is in the beauty of a sunrise, the silent wind that bends a hemlock, a stranger's smile, the splendor of an artistic masterpiece, the final moments of a loved one, the gentle nudging of conscience, the elegant orderliness of the physical universe.

God is even in the midst of the red light district.

When speaking among themselves, worshipers in Amsterdam's secret church referred to it by the code word "hart," a reference to its builder's name. In this sacred place, hidden in plain sight, they knelt before their

God. Their story reminds us to heed the yearning of our own hearts to discover and kneel before the places where God hides in plain sight.

# Poetry is God's Language

There are few books more delightful than *A History of the English Church and People* written in the eighth century by a Saxon monk named Bede.

I'm guessing that some readers might think nothing could be more boring than history, unless maybe it's church history. But Bede's style is so engaging, and the stories he spins are so lively, that his book is as pleasing as a good novel.

And as a bonus, it's also spiritually insightful.

In his book, Bede recounts many wonderful stories of miracles, pious kings, austere saints and devout abbesses and abbots. But for my money, his most intriguing tale is about a poet named Caedmon, who lived in Northumbria (modern-day Yorkshire) in the seventh century. Caedmon is often called the Father of English Sacred Song because his one surviving verse is probably the oldest poem in Old English to come down to us.

As Bede tells the story, Caedmon was an unlettered laborer who went largely unnoticed for a good part of his life. He was also shy, regularly fleeing feasts in his master's great hall if asked to join in the merrymaking with a song, which in seventh-century Northumbria meant a chanted verse accompanied by simple melodies plucked on a six-string harp.

One night Caedmon dreamt that a man asked him for a song. Caedmon replied that he didn't know how to sing. When the man in his dream insisted, Caedmon (who must have been feeling some dream panic at this point) stammered, "What should I sing?" "Sing about the creation of all things!" was the reply. Immediately, and to his utter surprise, Caedmon burst into a verse-song in his dream. When he awakened, he not only remembered what he'd chanted, but spontaneously added verses.

In offering a Latin rendering of Caedmon's Old English, Bede apologetically noted that poetry "cannot be translated literally from one language

## Poetry is God's Language

into another without losing much of its beauty and dignity." But even in translation, Caedmon's verse is magnificent:

> Praise we the Fashioner now of Heaven's fabric,
> The majesty of his might and his mind's wisdom,
> Work of the world-warden, worker of all wonders,
> How he the Lord of Glory everlasting,
> Wrought first for the race of mortals Heaven as a roof-tree,
> Then made he Middle Earth to be their mansion.

After his dream breakthrough, poems flowed out of Caedmon. Bede tells us that he could turn even the most ordinary experiences "into such melodious verse" that whoever heard them was enchanted. Then Bede says something especially worth heeding: "Caedmon did not acquire the art of poetry from any human, but received it as a free gift from God."

Bede's claim that poetry is God's gift is well said. Much of the world's sacred texts are verse-songs inspired, so the faithful believe, by revelation. The Hebrew Psalms, the Christian Magnificat, the Buddhist Diamond Sutra, entire sections of the Hindu Upanishads, Quranic verses, and indigenous chants: all are examples of how religious insights are poetically communicated.

Poetry, it might be said, is God's language, and the best medium for connecting with and celebrating God is the rhythmic poetry of liturgy, hymn, and sacred text.

For good reason. Straightforwardly descriptive language about the things in life that are most precious to us always falls short. But evocative language, the language of metaphor and simile, is better suited to convey their depth and richness.

Take, for example, our desire for God. We can straightforwardly say "I want God," but this is a lifelessly deflationary way of speaking about such a poignant longing. On the other hand, the psalmist's "As the deer pants for water, so my soul pants for thee, O God!" or the Song of Songs author's "Would that thou (God) would kiss me with the kisses of thy mouth!" beautifully capture the intensity of our yearning for the Divine.

Perhaps one of the reasons religion is on the decline in our culture is a dwindling appreciation of poetry. If verse is God's language, losing our ear for it deafens us to sacred texts as well as to poets who, like Caedmon, are God's oracles. Without verse-singers, our hearts wither and our landscapes become barren.

This cautionary insight alone makes reading Bede worthwhile.

# Naked Intent

If you visit the Pinacoteca, one of the magnificent galleries in the Vatican, you'll run across a painting by the high Baroque master Guido Reni.

History hasn't been kind to him. His name is largely forgotten by all but art historians. But one of his canvases, "St. Matthew and the Angel," is a genuine masterpiece.

In it, Reni depicts a white-haired Saint Matthew, quill pen in hand, expectantly leaning in to listen as an angel dictates the Gospel that bears Matthew's name. But what makes the painting so distinctive is that the communication between the two clearly isn't vocal. Their mouths are closed. Matthew and the angelic messenger of the Lord (the Greek *angelos* means "messenger") stare penetratingly at each other's face as if their very thoughts are being telepathically transmitted. The intensity of their eye-to-eye connection is palpable.

I don't know if Reni ever read a fourteenth-century mystical treatise entitled *The Cloud of Unknowing*. Chances are good he didn't. But his painting is nevertheless a pictorial paraphrase of the book's central message: "Think only of God. A naked intent toward God, the desire for God alone, is enough."

A naked intent, a focused reaching-out unsullied by ignoble motives, unworthy desires, or a thousand and one distractions: this is exactly what Reni captured in the piercingly alert way his Saint Matthew attends to the messenger of God. All God-believers long (or at least ought to long) for this kind of connection with the Divine. But how is it achieved? How can we who live in the blooming, buzzing world possibly hope to focus so intensely on God? Are we capable of resisting the pull and push of life long enough to attend single-mindedly to the Divine?

We are, but it takes some work. To a tiny handful of us—the saints who dwell, usually anonymously, in our midst—a naked intent toward God comes easily. But the rest of us have to work our way into it with steady and prayerful discipline. We must accept the herculean task of renouncing our idolatrous fixation on self. We must shift our focus of attention, our naked intent, from ourselves to the Divine.

All three Abrahamic religions have seasons in which the faithful are called to do just that. Jews fast, pray, and repent on the Days of Awe that culminate in Yom Kippur. Christians do likewise in Lent, and Muslims in Ramadan. These holy seasons are opportunities for us to draw nearer to God by clearing away the obstacles our own self-will puts in our way. They're crash courses in cultivating the naked intent toward God portrayed in Reni's masterpiece and recommended in *The Cloud of Unknowing*.

But just as a musician must constantly practice her art lest she lose proficiency in it, so we must continue our practice of focused straining toward God outside of holy seasons. Despite our good intentions, many of us lose focus and begin to drift back to our old ego-centered lives once Yom Kippur, Lent, and Ramadan end. And so we have to begin anew a year later. By then, of course, the cleansing will be even more difficult because we'll have added ten or eleven more months of self-worship and desire-indulgence to our lives.

So it's wise, after the seasons of repentance have run their course, to set aside one day of the week—the Lord's Day, the Sabbath—to continue cultivating a naked intent toward God. Without at least one day that interrupts the week's busy schedule, we risk settling back into old ego-driven habits. Keeping the Sabbath is a regular reminder of what we yearn for: closer and closer communion with God. It's a holy time that energizes our yearning for God by encouraging the withdrawal from ego and the renewal of spirit that we associate with Yom Kippur, Lent, and Ramadan.

After a few years of accustoming ourselves to nakedly intending toward God at least once a week and daily during holy seasons, the miracle happens. We reach the point where our focus on God is as piercing as Reni's Saint Matthew's and as lovingly intimate as the *Cloud*'s author says it should be. What once demanded laborious self-discipline now becomes effortless joy. What once was an on-and-off relationship with the Divine becomes as perpetual and intense as the communion shared by the angel and Saint Matthew.

Then all our seasons, and all our days, are holy.

# Luke's Icon

The great city of Constantinople, ancient Christendom's crown jewel, successfully repulsed some twenty-four major sieges throughout its 1,123-year history. But in 1453, Mehmet II, sultan of the Ottoman Empire, crashed through its defenses to claim it for Islam.

It took a full two months before Mehmet's gigantic cannons managed to breach the double walls that protected the city. The ensuing slaughter and destruction were terrible. The sultan allowed his troops to plunder the city for three days before calling a halt to the rampage. Churches, palaces, and homes were ransacked, women violated, and thousands of the city's citizens murdered or enslaved.

One of the casualties was Constantinople's magnificent basilica, Hagia Sophia. Its massive doors were battered down, its priests murdered, and its ornate crosses, gilded mosaics, and bejeweled reliquaries looted and carried off by soldiers.

One of the holy treasures that disappeared during those horrible three days was the Hodegetria, a life-size icon that depicted the Virgin Mary holding the Christ Child in her left arm and pointing to him with her right hand. Hodegetria means "she who shows the way." The icon was intended to demonstrate that Jesus is "the Way."

What made the Hodegetria so precious was that it had been painted according to a centuries-old tradition by the evangelist Luke. Eudokia, wife of the Byzantine emperor Theodosius II, had brought the Hodegetria to Constantinople from Jerusalem sometime in the early 400s.

We're reasonably confident of a handful of historical facts about Luke. He was a Greek physician who became a close associate of Saint Paul, accompanying him on some of his mission trips. Luke wrote the Gospel named after him as well as the Acts of the Apostles; taken together, they're the lengthiest New Testament document written by a single author.

## Luke's Icon

We can infer a few more facts about Luke from his Gospel.

Women play a larger role in his account of the life of Jesus than they do in the other three Gospels, indicating that he fully appreciated their importance to the early church. In his Gospel, he clearly empathizes with social outcasts and the materially poor. In his version of the Sermon on the Mount, for example, he has Jesus say "Blessed are the poor" instead of the Matthean "Blessed are the poor in spirit." Finally, Luke especially emphasizes the work of the Holy Spirit in his Gospel, suggesting that he was a man of deep prayer and inspiration.

Was he also an artist? Did he actually paint the Hodegetria? We have no way of knowing. But it's clear from the prominence of Jesus's mother, Mary, in Luke's Gospel that he was devoted to her. If Luke indeed possessed artistic talent, it's not unreasonable to suppose that the Holy Spirit would've inspired him to paint her image.

At any rate, he's long been recognized as the patron saint of artists.

On the day before Constantinople fell, the Hodegetria was carried in solemn procession around Hagia Sophia in the fervent hope that the Mother of God would intervene to rescue the besieged city. Thousands of people, including Constantine XI Palaeologus, the final Byzantine emperor, walked behind the icon, barefoot, weeping, and confessing their sins.

But to no avail. Mehmet took the city, and according to legend, the Hodegetria was chopped into pieces by looters. Over the centuries, various churches in Europe have claimed to possess this or that portion of the original icon, but their claims are doubtful.

Luke's icon wasn't the only relic dismembered when Constantinople fell. The evangelist, who died around 150, had been buried in Thebes originally. Two centuries later, his remains were transferred to Constantinople. During the siege, when it became clear that the city would be taken, Luke's relicts were divided and sent to Thebes, Padua, and Prague for safekeeping. They remain there still.

# The Real da Vinci Code

Holy Week's Maundy Thursday is a commemoration of the Last Supper, that final gathering of Jesus and his closest companions before his arrest and execution.

At the Last Supper, Jesus not only instituted the sacrament of Communion ("This is my body, this is my blood"), but also gave his followers a command that summed up everything he'd tried to teach them during their time together: "Love one another as I have loved you." "Maundy" is most likely a derivative of the Latin *mandatum*, or "command."

The Last Supper is also the event from which one of Jesus's companions, the embittered Judas, abruptly departed to sell him out. Holiness and sin, loyalty and betrayal, fellowship and alienation: these are the antipodal themes embedded in the story of the Last Supper.

They're the same antipodes that frame our lives, too.

For centuries, visual artists have struggled to capture the poignancy of the final meal shared by Jesus and his disciple in paintings, woodcuts, and sculptures. But there's no better-known depiction of the Last Supper than Leonardo da Vinci's. His late fifteenth-century painting became even more famous following the 2003 release of novelist Dan Brown's entertaining but utterly fanciful thriller *The Da Vinci Code*.

One of the reasons da Vinci's "Last Supper" is so compelling is that it's completely free of clichéd piety. Da Vinci certainly believed in God, but found the institutional Christianity of his day distastefully platitudinous and corrupt. Priests, he wrote, are full of sweet-sounding words that "promise paradise," all the while "trading in tricks and simulated miracles, duping the foolish multitude."[1] Living on the cusp of the Reformation as he

---

1. Richard Abanes, *The Truth Behind the Da Vinci Code* (Eugene, OR: Harvest, 2005), 65.

did, da Vinci believed, as Martin Luther would a few years later, that the church had transformed Christ into a marketable commodity.

In painting the Last Supper, then, da Vinci had two goals. First, he wanted to strip the scene of churchy artistic conventions. Second, he wanted his work to be a visual parable of what he saw as the church's faithlessness. So he focused on the moment in which Jesus announced to his disciples that one of them would shortly betray him.

Earlier artistic renderings of the Last Supper had piously encircled the heads of Jesus and his faithful disciples with glowing halos. Judas, however, was always haloless and typically distanced from Jesus and the others.

In da Vinci's "Last Supper," there are no halos at all. The only hint of one is the light around Jesus's head that comes from an open window behind him. Judas, far from being shunted off to a dark corner, is at table with the other disciples, actually seated closer to Jesus than half of his comrades. He's unidentifiable except for the unobtrusive money purse in his right hand, a reference to the thirty pieces of silver bounty for betraying Christ.

The genius of da Vinci's depiction of the Last Supper is his transformation of a biblical scene into a humbling spiritual lesson for viewers. His skill in working the antipodes of loyalty and betrayal, holiness and sin, and fellowship and alienation into a single painting jars us into the recognition that the same opposing impulses reside in us and in the church, often so intertwined that untangling them seems impossible.

We all find ourselves yearning for the Holy, longing to love as God loves us, to serve others with the selflessness of Jesus. Yet we're also susceptible to the Judas temptations of cynicism, self-glorification, and betrayal. The good in us nestles side-by-side with the evil, just as da Vinci's faithless Judas is cheek-to-jowl with the loyal disciples. This inner tension is part of what we're invited to remember on Maundy Thursday.

In one of his drawings, da Vinci famously depicted "Vitruvian Man," the figure of a male with legs and arms outstretched. It was intended as an illustration of human proportionality. Da Vinci's "Last Supper" might easily be called "Antipodal Humanity," depicting as it does our spiritually misproportioned ping-ponging from one extreme to the other.

Yet presiding at da Vinci's "Last Supper" is the One who liberates us from the tug-of-war between our antipodal tendencies.

Therein lies the painting's real message. That's the authentic da Vinci code.

# Ragged Edges

In the opening years of the twentieth century, certain philosophers dreamt of eliminating ambiguity from conventional language by replacing words with logical symbols that corresponded in an exact one-to-one way with facts.

Doing so, they believed, would purge thinking of needless confusion by eliminating the possibility of misstatement or misinterpretation.

The project soon ran out of steam, with all but diehards acknowledging that to expunge ambiguity from language was to throw out the very linguistic tools—allusive metaphors, similes, and analogies—that make language expressively rich and imaginatively creative.

One philosopher who changed his mind was an eccentric Austrian named Ludwig Wittgenstein. He arrived at the conclusion that both the world and language are much more complex than he and his fellow logicians had believed. So when it came to our efforts to speak about reality, he concluded that "what is ragged must be left ragged."

The real challenge was to convey the "indefiniteness" of certain human experiences "correctly and unfalsified into words."

Wittgenstein realized that religion is one of those areas of human experience so indefinite that it shouldn't be forced into language that seeks to smooth out its ragged edges. If we try to eliminate its ambiguity, we risk jettisoning the sense of mystery, awe, and wonder that religious speech properly evokes through metaphor and poetry. Language can only gesture at the Divine. God refuses to be domesticated by straightforwardly descriptive speech.

The Welsh poet R. S. Thomas (not to be confused with his better-known countryman Dylan Thomas) respected the impossibility of freeze-framing God in language. For Thomas, a priest in the Church of Wales, faith can never be described adequately enough to resist all criticism or skepticism. At its heart is the intuition that the universe is friendly rather than indifferent, or malevolent and God-filled rather than empty.

But because the human mind is simply incapable of fathoming God, all theological, philosophical, and even liturgical efforts to speak about God fall short. They're "imaginative" truths, said Thomas, poetic expressions of longing and love that offer glimpses of the Divine but are unable to do more. Nor does the claim that God became human in the person of Jesus make us better able to communicate who and what God is. If anything, it only deepens the mystery.

Thomas sought to communicate the essential unfathomability of God in his verse. He wrote, for example, that God

> Was too big to be nailed to the wall
> of a stone chapel, yet still we framed him
> between the boards of a black book.[1]

In his estimation, institutional Christianity tries so hard to define or explain God that faith, losing both mystery and challenge, becomes unhealthily comfortable.

> We have over-furnished
> our faith. Our churches
> are as limousines in the procession
> towards heaven.[2]

Yet Thomas was a steadfast believer in the tenets of his faith. His poetry was intended as an affirmation, not a denial, of God. As he once said of himself, "I believe in God. I'm trying to show how people sometimes attempt to pin down this Being who's not a being."[3]

Language can more or less describe "beings," objects or relationships in the world. But it can't stretch far enough to unambiguously describe Being itself. Only metaphor and simile will do, and even they necessarily fall short.

As Saint Paul said centuries ago, we see through a glass darkly when it comes to God. Four hundred years later, Saint Augustine made the same

---

1. R. S. Thomas, "A Welsh Testament," in *Collected Poems, 1945–1990* (London: Dent & Sons, 1994), 117.

2. R. S. Thomas, untitled poem, in *Counterpoint* (Newcastle-upon-Tyne, UK: Bloodaxe, 1990), 37.

3. Barry Morgan, *Strangely Orthodox: R. S. Thomas and His Poetry of Faith* (Llandysul, Wales: Gomer, 2006), 51.

## Part 6: Behold the Beauty

observation more forcefully. If we think we know God with clarity and precision, he wrote, we don't. Our knowledge of God is necessarily ragged; so is the language with which we struggle to say something about God. And that's how it should be, even though biblical literalists and dogmatists choose to ignore the point.

For Thomas, there's another reason why language can't peg God down. He believed that God remains deliberately elusive so as not to force himself on us. God comes to us

> unannounced
> remarkable merely for the absence
> of clamor,[4]

to invite rather than coerce a response from us.

The invitation is subtle, usually hidden away "unannounced" in the busy everyday world. It's up to us to attune ourselves to its

> speaking in the vernacular
> of the purposes of the One who is.[5]

These sorts of messily ragged-edged but wonder-filled encounters, which we experience but can't adequately put into words, are the stuff of which both faith and poetry are made.

---

4. R. S. Thomas, "Suddenly," in *Laboratories of the Spirit* (London: Macmillan, 1975), 201.

5. R. S. Thomas, "Suddenly," in *Laboratories of the Spirit* (London: Macmillan, 1975), 201.

# Starry Night, Golden Sun

In just ten years, he painted hundreds of portraits and landscapes. Although he died penniless, his artwork now commands astronomical prices.

Nor is he just for the wealthy. There are knockoffs of his stuff adorning posters, mugs, refrigerator magnets, stationary, mouse pads, umbrellas, and just about anything else you can think of. His life has been dramatized in two feature films and at least one novel. There's even a 1970s pop song about him.

He's probably the world's most recognizable painter.

I'm referring, of course, to Vincent van Gogh, a God-intoxicated artist whose work from first to last is intensely spiritual. Even a cursory inspection of his voluminous correspondence reveals that Vincent saw traces of God everywhere in the world and struggled mightily to express them through his paintings and drawings.

As a young man, before he realized that his true calling was art, Vincent served as a Christian lay minister to poverty-stricken miners in Belgium. It wasn't enough for him to preach the gospel to them. He felt the need to share their hard life in imitation of the "Son of Man who has no place to lay his head."

But prim church officials, alarmed at Vincent's show of solidarity with the down-and-out masses, quickly decided that he lacked the gravitas of a proper churchman and canned him.

This was the beginning of Vincent's disillusionment with institutional Christianity, but not with God. Even in Belgium, he'd believed that the Divine was more likely to be found in the concrete world than in abstract doctrines.

His transition from lay minister to artist was inspired by that conviction.

## Part 6: Behold the Beauty

"I'd like to paint men and women," Vincent wrote his brother Theo, "with that *je ne sais quoi* of the eternal, of which the halo used to be the symbol."[1]

Vincent did wind up producing a handful of "halo"-themed paintings: the Good Samaritan parable, the biblical story of Jesus resurrecting Lazarus, and the Pietà. Interestingly, he superimposed his own facial features onto the victim waylaid by robbers, the risen Lazarus, and the dead Jesus, suggesting that he identified in one way or another with each of them.

But for the most part, he glimpsed hints of the Divine in ordinary, everyday people and events. Earthbound peasants gathered around a table to share a simple meal of potatoes; lonely men sitting in a bar; the wistful Dr. Gachet, one of Vincent's physicians; farmers returning home at the end of the day's labor: Vincent saw the nimbus of the Eternal glowing around each of them, and invited us to see it too.

Nor was it only his human models who exuded an elusive *je ne sais quoi* aura of holiness. All of creation did. Vincent gazed up at starry night skies, experienced the sometimes comforting and sometimes frightening infinite depths of God, and expressed both by painting radiant pinwheels set in motion by a divine hand. He baked under the shimmery heat of a southern sun and painted huge yellow disks whose blazing brilliance lit up wheat fields and sunflowers to proclaim God's outpouring of grace.

When Vincent painted jet-black crows flying low over harvested fields of golden wheat, he saw them as emblems of the mysterious partnership of beginnings and endings, light and darkness, creation and destruction, fallenness and redemption. When he watched the birth of a calf and was moved by the tenderness with which its mother caressed it, he saw a replay of the Nativity.

When he filled his canvas with images of tall and slender cypresses, he did so because he sensed in them the Godward straining of all creation. Everything, no matter how common—a pair of worn shoes, a packet of tobacco resting on a chair, a vase of broken-stemmed sunflowers—whispered and occasionally shouted to him of God.

Even the brilliant colors he splashed with abandon onto his canvases—rich golds, saffron yellows, jewel-like azures, intense violets, blaring vermilions—were intended to draw attention, sometimes in quite breathtaking ways, to the presence of the Eternal in the here-and-now.

---

1. Vincent van Gogh, "Letter to Theo van Gogh, 3 September 1888," in *The Complete Letters of Vincent van Gogh, Vol. 3* (Boston: Little, Brown & Co., 1991), 25.

Jesus often used parables to communicate truths about God. Vincent, too, was a parabolist whose mission, as he put it, was to capture what "remained eternally true in the religion of Christ."

But whereas Jesus spoke his parables, Vincent painted his.

We—and God, too, for that matter—are indescribably richer for it.

# PART 7

# Mosaic of Beliefs

# The Scandal of Scientific Illiteracy

You can do science without theology, but it doesn't work the other way around. It's impossible to theologize well without taking into consideration what science tells us about physical reality. People of faith need to embrace this truth instead of hanging on to the delusion, too often encouraged by theologians, that it's possible to speak about God cogently while remaining scientifically illiterate.

Science, when done properly, is a methodology that restricts itself to an exploration and codification of natural phenomena and physical laws, and it does this extremely well. Making grandly sweeping statements about reality as a whole isn't science's job, as much as some scientists (think Carl Sagan or Neil DeGrasse Tyson) would like it to be. Scientists who ignore this violate their own methodology by making claims that simply can't be scientifically verified. They overstep the proper boundaries of their discipline.

Scientists don't need theology because their only proper object of study is the physical realm. But theology strives to say something intelligible about God, and that can only be done if the physical realm as well as the spiritual one is examined. If God created physical reality, then surely certain clues about the Creator are embedded within it. But without an understanding of basic science, how can they be discerned?

So theologians must understand how the physical realm works. They need science. Yet most mainstream theologians in all three Abrahamic traditions typically bypass correlating their thoughts about God with what science reveals about the God-created cosmos. I suspect that much of this scientific illiteracy is traceable to the long war of ideas between reason and faith or science and religion.

The seeds of that struggle were planted in the thirteenth century, when the philosophical works of Aristotle were introduced to Christian Europe. Because much of what Aristotle defended—the claim, for example, that

## Part 7: Mosaic of Beliefs

the universe was uncreated—ran counter to Christian, Jewish, and Muslim doctrine, many theologians rejected Aristotle outright. Others more sympathetic to the Greek philosopher's understanding of reality tried to hedge their bets by formulating what came to be known as the doctrine of double truth: reason provides one kind of legitimate truth, and faith provides another. Both are legitimate even if they clash with or even contradict one another.

Neither strategy worked well. Medieval theology that ignored Aristotelian analysis of the physical world became increasingly abstruse, and the double truth doctrine, essentially a Hail Mary pass, made no sense. How could two incompatible claims both be true? So battle lines between science and religion were quickly drawn.

In the early seventeenth century, the struggle between science and religion picked up steam, with the church's silencing of Galileo becoming the iconic example of religion's distrust of science.

The eighteenth-century Enlightenment, whose free-thinking luminaries were confident that science would liberate humanity once and for all from religious "superstition," ratcheted up the battle between religion and science to a new intensity. Then followed what many considered to be religion's deathblow: evolutionary theory, systematized in Darwin's 1859 *Origin of Species*.

The flashy but not terribly informed attacks on religion made in our own day by celebrity atheists are the latest skirmishes in the war between science and religion. As the incurably choleric Richard Dawkins insists, "not only is science corrosive to religion; religion is corrosive to science. It teaches people to be satisfied with trivial, supernatural nonexplanations."

The unfortunate legacy of this bad blood between religion and science is that theologians, who should be mining science for new insights into God's creation, tend to shy away from it. This is a distressingly missed opportunity to ask important questions. If life on earth is best understood in evolutionary terms, how ought that affect our understanding of God? What theological insights can be gleaned from Einstein's general relativity theory? What does the astounding unpredictability of subatomic activity suggest about God? What information can neuroscience and medicine give us about religious experience?

## The Scandal of Scientific Illiteracy

A millennium ago, Saint Anselm of Canterbury stated that the theologian's proper motto is *credo ut intelligam*, "I believe so that I may understand." Anselm knew that theology is both compatible with and actually complements science. But since his day, the motto has scandalously devolved into "I ignore science so that I may believe," and this is bad news indeed for theology.

# Denying Evolution

In all honesty, I'm not sure which is worse: creationist Christians who eschew reason by denying evolution, or liberal ones who claim to accept evolution but then, surprisingly, ignore it.

The first is damaging because it conveys the false message that Christianity is so out of touch with science that no rational person can or should take it seriously. The second harms by giving the equally inaccurate impression that Christian faith amiably coexists with evolution just so long as both are locked away from one another in airtight compartments. Creationists doggedly proclaim that evolution is a myth because the Bible tells them so. For the most part, evolution-accepting Christians act as if evolution is a fifth wheel, and really doesn't need to be incorporated into their religious worldview.

Creationist Christians are forthright deniers of evolution; liberal ones tend to be de facto deniers.

First, there are the creationist naysayers. A whopping 64 percent of white evangelicals and half of all black ones reject evolution. A third of Hispanic Roman Catholics, a full quarter of white ones, and 15 percent of white mainline Protestants believe that humans and all other species were simultaneously created ten thousand years ago.[1]

Chances are good that most creationist attacks on evolution are based on willful ignorance. The deniers simply haven't bothered to learn anything about the science they repudiate. Instead, they uncritically swallow the canned denunciations their pastors spoon-feed them, refusing to consider the mountains of geological evidence that dates the earth at nearly five

---

1. Pew Research Center, "Public's Views on Human Evolution," https://www.pewforum.org/2013/12/30/publics-views-on-human-evolution/, para. 6, Table 2.

billion years, and the equally compelling paleo-biological evidence for the evolution of species.

By contrast, de facto deniers pay lip service to evolution, but can't quite figure out how to fit it into their Christian convictions. "Evolution is God's way of creating life," they vaguely say, or "evolution is part of the divine plan," as if vanilla statements like these actually convey something meaningful about the intersection of faith and evolution.

They don't. If God indeed is the creator of everything, to say that evolution is part of God's plan is true but trivial. It explains nothing.

In our day and age, theologians are tasked to find ways of expressing Christianity's truth that are compatible with what science tells us about the physical order. After all, if the universe in which we live is truly God-created, nothing that we learn about it can be incompatible with belief in God. Yet except for a handful of exceptions—the twentieth-century Jesuit paleontologist Pierre Teilhard de Chardin comes immediately to mind here—few theologians have tried to synthesize the Christian worldview and evolutionary theory. Instead, they give a pro forma nod to it and then move on.

But this is foolish. Evolution isn't just idle speculation. It's as received a part of the cosmic story as the theory of relativity, and no person of faith can afford either to deny it or to act as if it needn't be taken into serious consideration when thinking about God and God's creation.

What, for example, does the indeterminacy of natural selection tell us about God? Might it be a physical parallel to the freedom God allows humans? Is there a moral lesson to be gleaned from the fact that God didn't create everything at once and for all time? Could it be a hint to us that both the physical cosmos and human existence are gradual unfoldings toward the cosmic crescendo that Teilhard de Chardin called the "Omega point"? If natural selection is random, what does it say about the God who injected it into physical reality? Might it suggest that God chooses not to micromanage natural phenomena? When did soul emerge in the evolutionary process, and what might its appearance tell us about our own spiritual journey?

These and scores of other questions that focus on the intersection of evolution and theology should be at the top of any theologian's to-explore list. Failure to grapple with them out of fear or ignorance transforms the Christian worldview into one that's hopelessly and unappealingly out of date. Not examining them also inhibits us from fully appreciating, as Darwin noted in the final paragraph of his *Origin of Species*, that "there is grandeur in this [evolutionary] view of life."[2] And although Darwin would probably disagree, a genuine synthesis of theology and evolution makes the view even grander.

2. Charles Darwin, "On the Origin of Species," in *The Portable Darwin*, ed. Duncan M. Porter and Peter W. Graham (New York: Penguin, 1993), 215.

# Fool's Gold

If you're one of those skeptics who insist that the whole religion thing is nothing but a crutch for timid people, you're in good company. Back in the 1920s, psychologist and confirmed atheist Sigmund Freud said the same thing, and offered it as a knockdown argument against the existence of God. Since then, it's become the skeptic's gold standard. Pick up anything written by the hottest celebrity atheists today, or surf atheist websites and blogs, and you're bound to run across it.

Here's what Freud says. To be human is to be perpetually frightened of violence, illness, natural disasters, and death, the mother of all fears. This chronic anxiety would have paralyzed both individuals and society if some psychological defense mechanism hadn't been found to help us cope. That's where religion comes in. It comforts us with the belief that there's a divine Parent who will protect us from everything we dread, just as mommy and daddy looked after us when we were kids.

This belief is delusional, however, because it's based on wishful thinking and—asserts Freud—any belief grounded even partly on what one wishes to be true is suspect. God-Believers desperately need for there to be a protective God-Father, and so they invent one. They believe what they want to believe because doing so succeeds, at least to some extent, in calming their fears. They confuse wishes with reality.

Freud concludes that what this means is that religious beliefs are neurotic illusions. God is nothing more than a product of wishful thinking. It's high time for humans to abandon their fantasies and step out into the clear light of reason.

Sounds compelling on the surface of things, doesn't it? Problem is, it's a terrible argument. There may be a strong case to be made for atheism. But this isn't it.

## Part 7: Mosaic of Beliefs

Freud and his atheist disciples go wrong because they fail to distinguish between the truth of a belief and its origin. The two are distinct, and to suppose that where or how a belief originates determines whether or not it's true is a logical fallacy.

Look at it this way. You and I have many beliefs which are true, and whose truth we can justify with rational arguments and evidence. But it's also possible to hold some true beliefs even when our reasons for believing them don't justify their truth in the slightest way.

I may believe that the movement of my fingers is connected with neuronal firings in my brain because microscopic dwarves inside my head are manipulating tiny gears. My belief that there's a causal connection between finger movement and brain firing is true, even though my reason for holding it is bizarrely false. Or I may believe that my significant other loves me because my own insecurity creates in me a desperate need to believe that I'm lovable. But this wishful thinking doesn't necessarily falsify my belief, because my significant other may in fact love me.

In other words, people can hold true beliefs for the wrong reasons.

Now think about Freud's argument. Even if we grant him his dubious initial assertion that religion is born of fear, and that consequently all belief in the existence of God is self-protective wishful thinking, this says nothing whatsoever about whether the belief that God exists is true or false. It might be a true one, even though people who accept it do so for bad or even bizarre reasons. Once again, the origin of a belief—in this case, wishful thinking provoked by fear—is distinct from the truth or falsity of a belief—that God exists.

What Freud gives us, then, is an insightful analysis of one of the many psychological motives that might incline a person to believe in God. But what he most definitely hasn't done is what he wanted: to offer a definitive argument against the existence of God. Of course some people use religion as a crutch or believe in God only because they're terrified of death. Many others doubtlessly believe in God because in their lonely sense of helplessness they need for there to be a benevolent God-Parent. But neither of these motives for God-belief says anything about the truth of God-belief.

All of which is to say that being in good company—in this case, Freud's—doesn't guarantee that the company you keep is correct. Atheists need to find themselves another gold standard.

# Heart Knowledge

*C'est le coeur qui sent Dieu et non la raison*, declared the seventeenth-century Christian theologian and mathematician Blaise Pascal. "It's the heart, not reason, that senses God."

Human reason, far from being at odds with faith, in fact tells us a great deal about God. But Pascal's observation is well worth heeding, because when it comes to knowing God, the heart properly leads the way. Reason maps the trail, but only after the heart blazes it.

There are some knowledge claims so obvious that any person with reasonable intelligence and five working senses immediately knows them to be true. Take, for example, logic's law of identity, which states that a thing is identical with itself. We need no special training to recognize its truth. Statements about physical phenomena that everyone regularly experiences are also pretty obvious. We don't require physics degrees to know that the sun rises in the east, things fall down and not up, water is wet, and so on.

Such truths are immediately accessible to everyone. We not only don't need specialized training to apprehend them; we don't need to be particularly moral or spiritual either. In fact, we can be downright immoral or coarsely unspiritual, and that won't affect our ability to know that A = A and water is wet. All that's requisite is common sense, experience, and memory.

But the world's religious traditions, including Christianity, contend that there are other truths which aren't as baldly obvious or accessible to everyone. Their discernment depends upon certain interior conditions being present in the knower: humility; attentiveness; an openness to wonder; qualities such as compassion, patience, and gratitude; and a capacity for all-embracing love.

The cultivation of these conditions demands resolute moral and spiritual disciplining of our will, thought, and actions, as well as commitment to regular and deep prayer. The goal is to liberate oneself, with help from

## Part 7: Mosaic of Beliefs

God and a faith community, from enslavement to the passions' ceaseless demands for ego-gratification. To the extent that we succeed, we approach what Jesus referred to in his Sermon on the Mount as "purity of heart."

Purity of heart bestows the spiritual clarity that accommodates a special kind of knowledge. It "opens the eyes of the heart," as the apostle Paul memorably put it, enabling a person of faith to apprehend evidence of the transcendent in the here-and-now that those who lack faith simply won't or can't discern. This heart knowledge doesn't make persons of faith superior to those without it. But it does sharpen their sensitivity to revelation, theophany, and miracle.

As Jesus promised, the pure in heart shall see God.

This insight is what Pascal had in mind when he said that the heart senses God. He knew that humans deeply yearn to commune with the Source of love from whom we spring and upon whom we depend for our continued existence. There's a connatural bond between us and God, preceding and indeed grounding any rational theological mapping.

Some of us misinterpret this yearning as desire for money, fame, or power, and others—the skeptics among us—pooh-pooh it as sloppy sentimentalism or superstition. But the pure of heart recognize the tug for what it is: an invitation for communion with God. Their purity gives them heart knowledge. Their hearts blaze a trail that remains hidden from skeptics.

Perhaps the most obvious scriptural authority for the importance of heart knowledge is a well-known episode from Luke's Gospel. Two persons distressed at the news of Jesus's crucifixion encounter a stranger as they journey to the village of Emmaus. They are "sullen-faced," their hearts shut down by grief, anger, and hopelessness.

The stranger initially reproaches them, albeit gently, for their foolish "slowness of heart." But as he continues to speak, they feel their hearts quickening—"burning within them"—until they suddenly know the stranger as the risen Christ. The relighting of their faith opens the eyes of their hearts. Only afterwards are rational efforts to comprehend and speak about the revelation possible or proper.

My guess is that Pascal meditated on this story's message again and again. As should we all.

# Pretend Believers

What I'm going to say here will likely startle some and rile others. But here goes: many of us who think we believe in God actually don't.

That includes lots of people who faithfully attend church, temple, or mosque, regularly read spiritual books, or jabber on and on about God at the drop of a hat.

It might include a fair number of clergy, too.

Human beliefs come in all shapes and sizes. I believe, for example, that I have a quickly graying beard, that Wales borders on England, that most pants have pockets, that the sun sets in the west, and that my family loves me. I'm confident that every one of these beliefs is most likely true, but I'm also confident that they aren't equally important.

The belief that I happen to have a beard, while true, is relatively insignificant when compared to my belief about the sun's behavior. If I find out next week that my understanding of modern fashion is hopelessly outdated and that most pants in fact don't have pockets, I won't be nearly as shocked as I would be to discover that my belief about my family's love is false. In the grand scheme of things, nobody much cares (I hope) whether pants have pockets, but everybody wants to be loved.

The general rule here is that our personal investment in our beliefs is proportionate to the weight of their content.

Many of our beliefs are relatively unessential to us. They hover on the periphery of our experience and consciousness, we rarely call upon them, and if we discover that one or two of them are false, it's no big deal. But others are quite important to us, intellectually as well as emotionally. We depend on them to get us through the day, and our world would rock if we discovered them to be false.

Now, consider belief in God. If God exists, then by definition nothing is more real than God or more vital for our own existence and, for that matter, for the universe itself. It follows that no belief we could possibly hold ought to be more personally invested in, more closely held, than our belief in God.

Belief in God isn't just another belief about just another fact in the world. It stands in a class of its own, and if we hold it, it should be the one belief that's absolutely central, the one belief upon which all our other beliefs ultimately rest, and the one that serves as the foundation for how we interpret the world and behave in it. We may be able to endure giving up other beliefs—even big ones, like the love of our family for us, that might crush us were we to lose them—but our belief in God ought to be so central to our well-being that to give it up would be to die, spiritually if not physically.

Yet look at the way things really are. How many people who say they believe in God are as deeply invested in it as all that? Not a lot, unfortunately.

All their other beliefs, not to mention actions, don't orbit around their belief in God. Instead, their God-belief too often is just another sidelined opinion they let into the game from time to time, but generally keep on the bench. Other beliefs inevitably usurp its importance: belief in themselves, in a loved one, in the value of money, and so on.

All this can be squeezed into a simple formula: if you claim to believe in God, but that belief isn't the most important one in your life, the one belief you couldn't survive without, then you may be fooling yourself. You may not really believe in God at all.

You may be a pretend believer.

This doesn't mean that someone who genuinely believes in God never goes through moments of doubt or confusion. But for him or her, such interludes are deeply agonizing, disorienting, and transient. For the pretend believer, they're little more than mild irritations. Those who lack real belief in God are incapable of religious despair at the thought that God might not be or that their faith may be faux.

# Double Standard

One of the oddities of skepticism is that otherwise rational opponents of religion often invoke a double standard in their assault on faith. It's not that they're intentionally dishonest or unfair, but that their extreme aversion to religion leads them into sloppy thinking. When hot emotion overtakes cool reason, hasty conclusions and bad arguments generally follow.

The double standard is embedded in the skeptic's objection to efforts to rationally argue for the existence of God. His predictable response is, "I won't believe in God unless you offer me proof that God exists!"

Now, proof is an intensely rigorous and unforgiving standard of appraisal. To prove a statement is to demonstrate its absolute, irrefutable certainty, such that no reasonable person can doubt it. If we use the word "proof" to mean something less than this, we don't really understand its definition.

It doesn't take a lot of life experience before we come to the realization that there are very few beliefs that can be justified in this irrefutable way, and that those which can tend to be remotely abstract and mathematical. The commonplace beliefs we rely on to get us through the day, not to mention the big ones that are especially near and dear to us, simply don't allow for absolute certainty.

We can't know with absolute, undoubtable certainty, for example, that our spouses love us. They may, after all, secretly find us repulsive, unworthy, or pathetic. Nor can we reasonably expect proof that the treatment our physician has suggested to us will definitely work, or that the shop where we regularly purchase our morning cup of coffee will be open tomorrow.

But the fortunate thing is this: we neither need nor require proof when it comes to such beliefs. Probability, based on a reasonable appraisal of available evidence and scrutiny of past experience, is more than adequate.

## Part 7: Mosaic of Beliefs

So even though we can't actually prove that our spouses love us, we may justifiably conclude that they most likely do on the basis of the kindness they show us, their loyalty to us in tough times, and so on. For anyone who isn't neurotic or fragilely insecure, this probable conclusion is good enough.

Or what about our doctor's recommendation of a course of treatment? Although we may desperately want rock-solid proof that it'll work, we ultimately decide for or against it by carefully weighing the evidence for its likelihood of success. What person in her right mind would refuse a promising medical therapy simply because it can't guarantee a cure?

When it comes to tomorrow morning's coffee, I can't prove that the shop where I always buy it will be there to serve me. After all, the building may burn down in the night or the owner may unexpectedly decide to take a holiday. But neither of those possibilities are likely. Much more probable is that the shop will be open for business on the morrow, like it's been every other day, and that I'll be able to get my usual coffee. Of course, I can't know this with absolute certainty, but who needs proof in this case? Probability is good enough.

The takeaway is that we humans are perfectly willing to accept probability as an acceptable standard for justified belief. If we held out for ironclad proof, we would paralyze ourselves with indecision and uncertainty.

Why, then, insist on proof when it comes to God? Why wouldn't a preponderance of evidence leading to a probable conclusion be sufficient, as it is for our other beliefs? Why reject any evidence—and there's quite a lot of it—that points to the probable existence of God simply because it doesn't add up to absolute certainty? Why demand a more rigorous standard of appraisal here than in most other situations?

Such a double standard makes no rational sense.

# Unintelligent Design

Let's get one thing straight right off the bat: if you believe in God, you accept that the universe was designed intelligently. But that's not the same as endorsing intelligent design (ID), the latest flashpoint in the old and tiresome war between religion and science.

ID argues that neo-Darwinian natural selection can't account for certain "irreducibly complex" biological phenomena. The only reasonable explanation for their existence is that God, the Intelligent Designer, inserted them into the evolutionary process by an act of special creation. Proponents insist that this is a legitimate scientific conclusion rather than a theological or faith-based one.

What does irreducible complexity mean? To explain it, ID defenders point to biochemical systems underlying light-sensing in eyes or clotting in blood. These systems, they argue, can't be accounted for by a gradual evolutionary accumulation of parts (in these cases, proteins) because all their components have to be present before the systems can operate. They must be complex from the get-go: hence their "irreducibility." But since such instant complexity defies the slow pace of natural selection, these biochemical systems must be special creations inserted into the evolutionary process to speed things up.

ID proponents are smart, and ought not to be confused with young-earthers who make awestruck pilgrimages to creationist museums to gawk at idiotic dioramas of Adam and Eve cavorting with dinosaurs. Still, nearly all biologists insist that ID is bogus science and that natural selection is perfectly capable of producing complex systems like the ones ID proponents focus on. The wrangling between ID champions and its critics has been nasty at times, culminating in the fiercely fought 2005 *Kitzmiller v. Dover School Board* case in which a US District Court in Pennsylvania concluded that ID is pseudoscience.

## Part 7: Mosaic of Beliefs

Truth be told, it's lousy theology too, because it undercuts its own case by unwittingly casting doubt on the intelligence of the Intelligent Designer. If you buy ID, you also have to buy that God is an occasional—well, bumbler. Here's why. ID's underlying assumption is that the universe is rational and orderly because it's the creation of a supremely rational and infallible deity. But ID's insistence on God's ad hoc intervention in the evolutionary process casts doubt on the rationality of God and the orderliness of the created order, implying as it does that sometimes God has to fiddle with a flawed universe to fix snafus that God should've foreseen.

It's an odd sort of rational and orderly universe that requires this kind of catchup patchwork, and an odd sort of Intelligent Designer who has to backtrack to correct mistakes. A supremely rational and infallible deity should never be in the position of having to say "Oops!" God shouldn't have to plug holes in the cosmic dike because there shouldn't be any holes to plug in the first place.

Does the failure of ID mean that God-believers are forced back into head-in-the-sand creationism? No, thank goodness. A viable alternative to both biblical creationism and ID is "theistic evolution," a theory which argues that faith and evolution are compatible. From this perspective, evolution is a very real physical process. But as part of a God-created universe, it's more than simply a material phenomenon. It's also a deeply purposeful, spirit-infused flow by which God continuously coaxes reality toward a richer physical, moral, and spiritual symbiosis.

Theistic evolutionists think of God as the divine Omega Point who uses the evolutionary process to lovingly draw all creation towards fulfillment. God isn't a Cosmic Fixer who occasionally plugs holes in physical evolution, much less a wizard who magically whips up a universe in six days. God is the Creator whose unquenchable vitality fuels evolution, and God is evolution's ultimate destination. The study of evolution—indeed, the study of any natural science—can and ought to be an act of piety.

Obviously, neither convinced atheists nor biblical fundamentalists—nor even ID defenders—are eager to embrace theistic evolution. But there are hopeful signs that old ways of thinking about the universe are beginning to change. Thomas Nagel, renowned philosopher and avowed atheist, recently announced that he now believes an exclusively materialistic interpretation of evolution makes no sense. It could be, he said, that Intelligence is at work in the universe after all.

Perhaps the war between science and religion is drawing to a close.

# Big Bang Boogie

"You don't believe in God?! But if there's no God, what caused the universe?"
"The Big Bang. No need to drag God into the picture."
"Ah-ha! But what caused the Big Bang?"
"Nothing."
"But how can something come from nothing?"
"It just did."

Chances are good that most of us have heard one version or another of this squabble about cosmic origins. The atheist claims that the Big Bang is a sufficient explanation for the universe's existence. The theist pushes back by insisting that Big Bang itself requires a cause.

There's merit in both camps. The atheist is correct when he claims that Big Bang adequately accounts for the creation of the physical universe. But the theist is right in her intuition that there's something implausible about a physical universe spontaneously generating.

Without both of these perspectives, the Big Bang just doesn't boogie.

Most everyone agrees that the Big Bang theory, first formulated in 1927 by Jesuit physicist Georges Lemaître (and resisted mightily for a time by Albert Einstein), is the best explanation of how the physical universe got here. Working backward from the measurable expansion rate of the universe, physicists theorize that nearly fourteen billion years ago an infinitesimal speck of energy with unimaginable density spontaneously appeared in a quantum vacuum, a state with the lowest possible energy level. The speck exploded or "inflated" outward to eventually form not only stars, planets, and galaxies, but space-time itself.

Atheists believe that Big Bang's something-from-nothing explosion is all there is to say about the universe's origin. British physicist Stephen Hawking, for example, insists that it accounts for how the "universe appeared spontaneously, starting off in every possible way." Cosmologist

Lawrence Krauss has made a career for himself by proclaiming that we live in "a universe created from nothing." Both of them scoff at questions that ask why Big Bang occurred in the first place. As twentieth-century philosopher and atheist Bertrand Russell once remarked, the universe simply is. Move on.

But things aren't that cut-and-dried. To claim that something suddenly emerges from absolutely nothing makes no sense in the physical realm, even at the subatomic level, where particles pop up and disappear again in unpredictable ways. So although we can accept Big Bang's hypothesis that the physical universe exploded from a primordial speck of dense energy, the question of how the speck emerged from nothing still remains. It simply can't be brushed away as easily as Russell thinks. That's because there's no logical bridge between nothing and something.

The truth of the matter is that the speck didn't spontaneously generate from nothing. To define a quantum vacuum as "nothing," as Hawking and Krauss do, is to ignore the Philosophy 101 fact that even a vacuum has being. It exists—it "ises"—if in no other way than as a state of pure potentiality. "No matter how mathematically or physically subtle the initial cosmic conditions may have been," observes theologian and cosmologist John Haught, "they still enjoyed some mode of being."

So the necessary condition for the Big Bang—being, a state of sheer existence laden with possibility—predated the explosion that created the universe. Embedded in pre-Big Bang being were the seeds of the laws that define physical reality.

The question then becomes: how is it that there is being at all, including the quantum vacuum in which the universe was birthed? Two possibilities emerge: being is eternal, or it's created by God.

The first possibility boggles the mind, leaving unresolved and unresolvable wonder-filled questions that we humans have felt called to ask from Day One: Why does reality exist? Why is there something rather than nothing? The more fruitful alternative, one dictated by reason as much as by faith, is to presume the existence of a divine Architect who created and sustained the raw being that in turn allowed for the Big Bang emergence of the universe. The difference between the two possibilities is stark. With the first, reality forever remains an impenetrable question mark. As Russell said, it just is. With the second, it becomes inexhaustibly explorable.

Big Bang offers us a good understanding of the physical "how" of the universe's origin, but gives no answer to its metaphysical "why." That's where being comes in. Big Bang can't boogie without being. Being precedes universe, and the best explanation of being is that it's created by God.

# Searching for Common Ground

Let's face it: theists and atheists are never going to agree on the God thing. There are occasional conversions in either direction—theists losing faith and atheists acquiring it—but for the most part, folks on opposite sides of the issue are content, out of conviction or inertia, to remain where they are.

Yet despite disagreeing about God, theists and atheists share a lot of beliefs. It's high time we acknowledged and celebrated them instead of focusing so exclusively on our differences. And even when we do disagree, we can discipline ourselves to "dispute without animosity," as Saint Augustine advised, "just as a person dialogues with him or herself."

An absolutely necessary condition for discovering our common ground is calling a halt to the snipes and snarks both camps lob at each other. Theists have to learn that most atheists aren't sharp-tongued haters of religion who go ballistic at the sight of a Christmas crèche. For their part, atheists need to admit that most theists aren't holier-then-thou, evolution-denying fundamentalists. Intemperate and ill-informed pugilists like Richard Dawkins and Christopher Hitchens no more represent thoughtful atheists than faux-Christian celebrities like Pat Robertson or Joel Osteen represent prayerful theists.

Another essential condition is that people in both camps actually make an effort to meet one another. It's astounding how little real contact theists have with atheists or atheists with theists. Both tend to associate with their own kind, and this of course only encourages mutual stereotyping. It's too easy to demonize people when we have no personal relationship with them. Face-to-face dialoguing would help atheists and theists alike to jettison caricatures of each other's convictions.

Once theists and atheists stop bickering long enough to listen to one another, the common ground becomes visible pretty quickly.

## Searching for Common Ground

First, both atheists and theists acknowledge that there's an ultimate mystery lying at the heart of the universe: the question of why reality exists at all. The atheist holds that Big Bang birthed the universe, and the theist believes that God created Big Bang. But neither can answer the fundamental question of why there's anything at all, including the Big Bang. Atheist astronomer Carl Sagan acknowledged as much. When we ask such a question, he said, "We know we are approaching the grandest of mysteries."[1] Einstein agreed: "The most beautiful experience we can have is the mysterious."[2] So atheists and theists share a humbling sense of wonder and awe when they contemplate the universe.

They also share profound gratitude. Both are thankful that they live in a universe which displays beauty and deep-down orderliness. The atheist marvels at evolution's intricacy, and the theist is wowed by what she believes to be God's handiwork in and through evolution. But both are grateful for the magnificence of the natural realm.

Atheist mathematician John Allen Paulos expressed this overwhelming sense of gratitude by saying that the best way he knows to give thanks for the "wonder of the world" in all its "intricacy, beauty, and mystery" is to utter a single-worded but heartfelt prayer: "Yeah!" This grateful affirmation of nature's majesty and mystery is echoed time and again in the Hebrew Psalms and, indeed, in all religious traditions.

Theists and atheists also share a sense of responsibility to care for the natural order. Both want to leave as light an environmental footprint as possible. Atheists are motivated by the sober realization that human greed and arrogance is capable of destroying the world. Theists believe that humans are appointed by God to be stewards or protectors of creation. But both are equally concerned to save the planet.

Finally, atheists and theists are humanitarians who believe that persons throughout the world are endowed with dignity and possess certain basic rights. Theists believe that these rights are ultimately grounded in God's moral law, while atheists appeal to secular moral standards. But both want to see the hungry fed, the oppressed liberated, and the victimized rescued.

The war of words between atheists and theists needn't continue if wiser heads and kinder hearts refuse to let the likes of Dawkins or Robertson hijack the conversation. All we need do is quit saying "No!" to one another long enough to focus on our commonly held "Yeahs!"

1. Carl Sagan, *Cosmos* (New York: Random House, 1980), 4.
2. Albert Einstein, *The World As I See It* (N.p.: Snowball, 2014), 16.

# When Science Oversteps

It's hard to imagine and frightening to contemplate where we'd be without science. Just about every aspect of our day-to-day lives has been improved by medicine, computers, engineering, chemistry, and physics. Granted, scientific research and technological innovation can give rise to undesirable consequences like weapons of mass destruction, pollution, and global warming. But the culprit here is human mismanagement, not science per se.

Science can even heighten our sense of wonder and beauty. If you doubt that, you've never taken a look at the images given us by the Hubble Space Telescope.

So science is a very good thing—as long as its practitioners don't try to push it beyond its proper limits. When they do that, they not only betray the very nature of science, but their misguided conclusions generate a good deal of mischief, if not outright harm.

The most obvious overstepping comes from celebrity scientists like Carl Sagan, Neil deGrasse Tyson, and Stephen Hawking (not to mention second-rate celebrity atheists like Richard Dawkins) when they insist that science shows, to use Sagan's famous dictum, that "the [physical] cosmos is all that is or was or ever will be," and that therefore God is a fiction. Even if that statement is true—and there's good reason to suspect it isn't—its assertion is way above science's pay grade.

Here's why.

Properly speaking, science operates according to what's usually called "methodological naturalism": only those explanations for phenomena which can be scientifically tested should be sought or accepted. This automatically precludes any hypothesis that rests in part or whole on nonnatural or nonphysical postulates. Testability, in turn, consists in observing natural or physical phenomena, formulating hypothetical explanations for them, predicting future occurrences based on those hypotheses, and testing the accuracy of the prediction.

Methodological naturalism isn't just a tool for scientists. You and I embrace it as a working assumption every time we go to a physician instead of a faith healer or consult the Weather Channel rather than a ouija board—yet more examples of how science enriches our lives.

So far, so good. The trouble arises when scientists like Sagan, Tyson, and Hawking violate methodological naturalism by insisting that science demonstrates that reality is nothing other than physical, and that it's self-originating, self-explanatory, and without overall purpose. Consequently, God-belief and all that it involves is an archaic superstition which ought to be consigned to history's dustbin. The universe, physical through-and-through, leaves no room for such nonsense.

But in saying this, Sagan, Tyson, and Hawking trample the proper boundaries of scientific investigation. Overall claims about the nature of reality itself simply aren't within science's purview, at least not if scientists remain loyal to the fundamental methodology by which science operates. To say that the cosmos is purely physical is, I suppose, a hypothesis. But from a properly scientific perspective, it's an excruciatingly bad one because it's one of those speculative postulates that's untestable, neither verifiable nor falsifiable by the standards of methodological naturalism.

It is, in short, a metaphysical claim that exceeds what science is qualified to investigate and evaluate. Science can and should explore discrete physical phenomena, and when it does so, we all benefit. But it needs to back off of judgments that go beyond its scope.

To paraphrase Clint Eastwood, a good scientist should know her limitations.

Does this mean that a scientist has no right to be an atheist? Of course not. Just like the rest of us, scientists are entitled to their opinions. There are even some scientists who, along with an astounding 38 percent of the American populace, hold the profoundly foolish belief that the earth is only ten thousand years old. But scientists who deny God's existence can't claim scientific warrant for their conviction.

At any rate, not if they wish to remain loyal to methodological naturalism.

# PART 8

# To Everything There Is a Season

# Stretching Forward (Advent)

The holy season of Advent is all about anticipation. *Adventus*, the word's Latin root, means a "coming" or an "approaching." In Advent, we Christians longingly await the birth, the coming, of the Christ Child.

But it isn't only we who wait. God waits too. And it isn't only God who is born. So are we.

Few people better capture the anticipation that's proper to Advent than the fourth-century Gregory of Nyssa, who takes as his starting point a passage from Paul's letter to the Philippians: "Forgetting what lies behind and straining forward to what lies ahead, I press on toward the goal for the prize of the heavenly call of God in Jesus Christ."

Paul's "straining forward" is a translation of the Greek word *epektasis*, which can just as easily be rendered "stretching out toward" or "reaching forward." Regardless of how it's translated, *epektasis* is the state of eagerly anticipating and moving toward God.

In his book *Life of Moses*, Gregory offers the eponymous lawgiver as an inspiration for those of us who yearningly strain forward toward God. "Moses," he writes, "as he was becoming ever greater, at no time stopped in his ascent, or did he set a limit for himself in his upward course."[1] Beginning with his burning bush encounter, Moses's spiritual journey led him closer and closer to the Divine for whom he yearned.

Yet Moses's straining forward never culminated in a face-to-face encounter with God. The closest he came was seeing God's back, not God's face. Consequently, as Gregory says, "although lifted up through such lofty experiences, Moses is still unsatisfied in his desire for more. He still thirsts for that with which he constantly filled himself to capacity, and he asks to

---

1. Gregory of Nyssa, *Life of Moses* §227.

## Part 8: To Everything There Is a Season

attain as if he had never partaken, beseeching God to appear to him, not according to his capacity to partake, but according to God's true being."

This is an interesting observation, implying as it does that no matter how much Moses yearns for God, and how "filled to capacity" he is with God, his stretching toward the Divine will always fall short of its goal, "God's true being." Even after death, Gregory suggests, we can't attain a direct experience of God. Our finitude simply doesn't allow it; we haven't the "capacity to partake" of infinity. We are but sponges, and God is a shoreless ocean. How could we possibly soak up Divine vastness?

And so we await God, which means that Advent is always. We're forever, both in this life and the next, yearning for closer and closer communion with God. In each stage of our yearning, we're transformed, reborn, as we draw nearer to God, even though we can never fully experience God's plenitude. Just as God forever births Christ—for, of course, the Christ-event is eternal—humans are reborn at each stage of our straining forward toward God.

Additionally, our waiting for God is paralleled by God's waiting for us. For just as we're incomplete beings in proportion to our distance from God, it's also the case that God is incomplete without us. That's because the primary bond between God and humans is love. Lovers who long to be with one another are unfulfilled if their union is frustrated.

Perhaps the best visual portrayal of the way God strains toward us and we toward God is the centerpiece of Michelangelo's Sistine Chapel ceiling: God lovingly, longingly, stretching his arm across infinity to touch the yearningly outstretched hand of Adam. Michelangelo meant the scene to depict the Genesis account of creation. But it's also a perfect icon of the mutual straining, the shared *epektasis*, that is the message of Advent.

It's easy during the Advent period of waiting to get jaded by the all-too-predictable set of accoutrements associated with the season: tacky Christmas pop songs ("I Saw Mommy Kissing Santa Claus"), commercials incessantly shouting as us to buy-Buy-BUY, over-the-top house and lawn decorations, and a resumption of the tiresome debate about whether one should say "Merry Christmas" or "Happy Holidays."

But we can insulate ourselves from all this if we embrace Advent as an opportunity to be especially mindful of our *epektasis*, our unfulfillable yet always rejuvenating yearning for God, and of the Divine Birth two millennia ago that stretches forward to perennially rebirth us.

# The Great O's (Advent)

Almost everyone is familiar with the carol "O Come O Come Emmanuel." But what you may not know is that the song is based on a beautiful series of ancient prayers called the O Antiphons—or, less formally, the Great O's.

I recommend them to you as a wonderful way to observe the final week before Christmas, the holy Feast of the Nativity of Our Lord. Because Christmas begins at sundown on December 24, Christmas Eve isn't counted as part of Advent; hence the O Antiphons begin on December seventeenth and end on the twenty-third, rather than the twenty-fourth.

An antiphon is a phrase that's said or sung before and after a psalm or canticle. There are antiphons specific to each of the church seasons. Their purpose is to capture the various spiritual timbres and messages of the seasons. Solemnly penitential antiphons that are appropriately sung during Lent, for example, would be out of place in the celebratory season of Epiphany.

The O Antiphons can be sung at any time during Advent's final week. Because they're easily memorized, I tend to whisper them throughout the day to keep myself mindful of the coming of the Messiah. But, strictly speaking, they typically precede and follow Evening Prayer's recitation of the Magnificat, the Song of Mary recorded in Luke's Gospel (1:46–55) that proclaims the liberating message of God's mercy and justice.

The O Antiphons are so-named because all seven of them begin with the word "O," immediately followed by one of the titles for the Messiah recorded by the prophet Isaiah. Running from first to last, the messianic titles celebrated in the antiphons are "Wisdom," "Ruler of Israel," "Root of Jesse," "Key of David," "Rising Dawn," "King of the Gentiles," and "Emmanuel."

## Part 8: To Everything There Is a Season

Just to give you a feel for the O Antiphons' beauty, here are both the English and the Latin versions of the third one, which is sung on December nineteenth.

"O Root of Jesse's stem, sign of God's love for all his people: come to save us without delay!"

"*O Radix Jesse, qui stas in signum populorum, super quem continebunt reges os suum, quem Gentes deprecabuntur: veni ad liberandum nos, iam noli tardare!*"

Each of the O Antiphons has the same structure: a proclamation of one of the Messiah's titles, brief praise, and a short petitionary prayer that's prefaced by the word "come" (Latin, *veni*). You can positively feel the quiver of anticipation in the antiphons' longing for the arrival of the Messiah, the Emmanuel who revitalizes creation with wisdom, power, love, liberation, justice, and salvation, and who shows us what it means to be fully human.

When we sing the O Antiphons, we participate in a centuries-old tradition. It's not clear when they were first used, but the early sixth-century philosopher Boethius alludes to them. Two centuries later, with the practice of Gregorian chant catching on in prayer and liturgy, the O Antiphons appear to have become staples in the many monasteries that were beginning to dot Europe.

Arranged in their final sequence by Benedictine monks during the Middle Ages, the first letters of the Latin titles of the Messiah in each of the O Antiphons, when read backwards, make an acrostic: *Ero cras*, or "Tomorrow I will be there." So, as more than one commentator has observed, the O Antiphons are at one and the same time a prayer—"Come!"—and, acrostically, an answer—"I will!"

All of us are painfully aware of how hectic, noisy, and deflationary our consumerist culture can make the Christmas season, and we long to recapture its simple and holy joy, gratitude, and wonderment. Calming the spirit by praying the O Antiphons is one very good way of doing that. Say them, chant them, or sing them, by yourself or with family and friends. Let their beauty prepare you for the birth of God.

# They Who Are Wisest (Christmas)

All the razzmatazz that we've come to associate with Christmas goes into full swing immediately after Thanksgiving. Merchants vie for our cash, radios blare seasonal music (much of it pretty awful), and the normal pace of life suddenly gears into overdrive.

But underneath all the glittery tinsel and consumer madness, the spirit of Christmas endures, as it always will. I know of few storytellers who more grippingly capture its essence than William Sydney Porter, better known as O. Henry, in his "The Gift of the Magi."

O. Henry introduces us to Jim and Della, a young married couple down on their luck. Jim's already meager income has been reduced even more by some unspecified misfortune, and the two find themselves teetering on the shabby border of poverty.

But each of them still owns one dearly cherished treasure. For Jim, it's a gold watch that belonged to his father and grandfather. For Della, it's her magnificent, waist-length hair.

Christmas is now upon them. Della knows that Jim has his heart set on a chain for his beloved watch, and Jim knows that Della yearns for some tortoise shell combs for the luxuriant hair she's so proud of. But they have no money.

So, unbeknown to one another, the two sacrifice their most treasured possessions. Jim pawns his watch to buy Della the combs, and Della sells her tresses to buy Jim the watch chain. On Christmas Eve, Jim joyfully rushes home with the combs, only to discover Della's close-cropped hair. Della, delighted at the prospect of pleasing Jim with the watch chain, quickly learns that her gift is equally useless.

Some might see this as a comedy of errors. But O. Henry knows it to be a profound expression of the Christmas spirit. "I have lamely related to you the uneventful chronicle of two foolish children who most unwisely sacrificed for each other the greatest treasures of their house," he writes. "But in a last word to the wise of these days let it be said that of all who give gifts these two were the wisest. Of all who give and receive gifts, such as they are wisest. Everywhere they are wisest. They are the magi."

Our English word "wise" derives from an ancient verb that means "to see" or "to envision." A wise person is someone able to look beneath the surface of things to discover their true and often hidden nature. The wise see further and deeper than the rest of us.

Think of the three magi in the nativity story. They looked into the night sky and saw the same nova that everyone else did. But while other folks merely gawked at it, the magi sensed its significance, and they sacrificed the comfort of hearth and home to seek out what it heralded. They wouldn't have undertaken such a long and dangerous trek just out of intellectual curiosity. Love drove them, because in their wisdom they recognized that the child they sought was destined to become the Light of the World. When they found the babe, they laid gold, frankincense, and myrrh before him. But the real Christmas gift they offered was their love.

Similarly, Della and Jim, wise beyond their years, deeply sensed the true meaning of Christmas. Other folks might scurry around looking for bargains. But like the magi at that first Christmas, O. Henry's young couple knew that the best gift of all is a love willing and even eager to give up what one most values for the beloved's sake. To a cynic, their sacrifice is folly and its outcome laughable. What could possibly be more useless than a chain without a watch or a comb without tresses? But when Jim saw Della's shorn head, and Della noticed Jim's empty watch pocket, they both knew that the gifts of love they exchanged were better than a thousand gold watches or hair luxuriant enough to make Rapunzel jealous.

This is the true spirit of Christmas: to sell all we have to buy the pearl of great price, and then to give it to another. We do so in celebration of the God who gladly relinquished Godhood so that all humankind might be ennobled by his loving sacrifice.

They who see this, and who strive to keep the wonder of it in their hearts during Christmas, are the wisest. Everywhere they are wisest.

# Yuletide Magic (Christmas)

In *Shadowlands*, the 1985 BBC drama about C. S. Lewis (not to be confused with the 1993 Hollywood grotesquerie of the same title), Lewis, played by veteran actor Joss Ackland, says something about Yuletide that rings true.

"Think of Christmas in terms of magic. The birth of a helpless, screaming creature who happens to be God. An omnipotent baby. The coming of new life in the heart of winter, when everything seems to be dead. The snow falls and the trees bear fruit. That's real magic."

Whether we cherish Christmas as a holy day or welcome it as a non-religious occasion to be with loved ones, most of us sense its enchantment. Compassion, kindness, patience, peace, and good will become more than mere words. For at least a while, we actually feel and live their truth. Even our frenetic gift-giving is a reflection of the joyful generosity awakened by the magic of Christmas.

All of us have favorite stories about Christmas magic. Here are four of mine.

On Christmas day in 1223, Francis of Assisi, inspired by Saint Luke's account of Jesus's birth and wanting to make the story come alive for his contemporaries, created the world's first Christmas crèche. He borrowed an ox, an ass, and some hay from a peasant, knocked together a rough wooden manger, and invited folks in the small town of Grecio to visit the crèche and hear him preach.

According to Saint Bonaventure, an early biographer of Francis, one of the villagers, a hard-bitten soldier, "affirmed that he beheld an Infant marvelously beautiful, sleeping in the manger." This is wondrous enough. But Bonaventure sensed an even richer bit of magic on that Christmas day: the crèche and Francis's preaching "excited all hearts" to a joyful recognition that the world is wondrously saturated with God's incarnate presence.

## Part 8: To Everything There Is a Season

Or take the heartwarming 1843 novella *A Christmas Carol*. Its author, Charles Dickens, wasn't a particularly religious man. But his story is a celebration of the magical beauty of Christmas that coaxes out the humanity of even loveless misers like Ebenezer Scrooge. Openhearted Bob Cratchit, brave Tiny Tim, and Scrooge's generous nephew Fred draw us into the same festive joy they awakened in Scrooge. Dicken's tale isn't a cheap feel-good story designed to manipulate our emotions. It's an homage to the fact, felt by millions throughout the centuries, that there's something about Christmas that delights and transforms even the roughest of us.

Then there's "A Child's Christmas in Wales," the beautiful prose poem recorded by Welsh author Dylan Thomas in 1952. In it, Thomas fondly remembers the Christmases of his childhood, when relatives would gather, uncles would eat too much, cousins would get into mischief snowballing the cats, and the whole world glowed with joy.

At the end of each magical Christmas, Thomas recalled, he would gaze through his bedroom window, "out into the moonlight and the unending smoke-colored snow. I could see the lights in the windows of all the other houses on our hill and hear the music rising from them up the long, steadily falling night. I turned the gas down, I got into bed, I said some words to the close and holy darkness, and then I slept."

Christmas magic can also occur in the unlikeliest of places.

Five months after the 1914 eruption of the conflict that came to be called World War I, German and British troops faced one another on the Western Front with only a narrow band of no man's land separating their trenches. On Christmas morning, Germans began singing carols. Before long, the Brits opposite them joined in. White flags of truce went up on both sides, and then the magic happened: soldiers who had believed themselves mortal enemies of one another climbed out of their trenches, shook hands, exchanged gifts of chocolate, tobacco, and spirits, and played football.

When the mustachioed commanders of both armies heard about the spontaneous Christmas truce, they were predictably furious. How could they run a respectable war if soldiers from either side celebrated Christmas together?! So the generals ordered that future fraternization with the enemy be harshly punished. But despite that, the magic of that Christmas glowed in the soldiers' hearts.

I wish each of you a generous share of Yuletide's magic. And as Tiny Tim said, "God bless us, everyone!"

# Rachel Weeping
## (Feast of the Holy Innocents)

In the Christian calendar, the eight days between Christmas and New Year's is known as the Octave of Christmas.

Given the season, you'd think it would be a festive time, and for the most part it is. But the Octave includes a somber couple of days which remind us that our joy should never blind us to the fact that there is genuine and sometimes horrific suffering in the world.

The first of these, Saint Stephen's Day, falls on December 26. Stephen, one of the first deacons in the early church, was cruelly stoned to death for the crime of proclaiming his faith.

The second, the Feast of the Holy Innocents, is on December 28. It recalls an atrocity, recorded in Matthew's Gospel, that took place shortly after Jesus's birth.

When the Magi told paranoiac King Herod about the birth of the Christ Child, he sent his thugs to Bethlehem with orders to murder all male children under the age of two. The slaughter was so cruel that it left Matthew at a loss for words. All he could think to do was quote a passage from the prophet Jeremiah, who, centuries earlier, grieved over the Assyrian conquest of Israel by imagining the spirit of Rachel, wife of the patriarch Jacob, weeping over the calamity that befell her children.

Rachel still has good cause to weep. Children across the globe continue to suffer in unspeakable ways, bringing ignominy to the Herods who harm them and those of us who do nothing to protect them.

According to UNICEF, the United Nations bureau dedicated to helping the world's children, Human Rights Watch, and Amnesty International, here are some of the sobering facts:

- Nearly 20 percent of the world's kids live in extreme poverty, defined by an income of less than two dollars per day;
- Three million children perish each year from malnutrition, while millions more suffer from stunted physical and mental development due to lack of sufficient protein;
- Half a million kids die each year from easily preventable or treatable diseases such as diarrhea, pneumonia, malaria, and tuberculosis;
- In the world's poorest nations, one in four kids, some as young as five years, labor under extreme or hazardous conditions;
- Forty-eight million children have been displaced from their homes by war, famine, drought, or natural disaster;
- A staggering one hundred million kids are estimated to live on the streets, scrounging a living by thievery, begging, or prostitution;
- In many war-torn developing nations, children are forcibly conscripted into militias to serve as soldiers, slaves, and prostitutes. Over the last decade, two million of them have been slaughtered in battle; six million severely wounded; and ten million psychologically traumatized.

Nor is the suffering of kids a tragedy to which our own nation is immune. Recently exposed scandals in the Roman Catholic and Jehovah's Witnesses communities shockingly reveal that sexual predation of American kids, even by religious leaders, is a dismaying reality.

Moreover, some 11.5 million kids in this country live in poverty, including an astounding 48 percent of rural children. An additional 1.3 million live hand-to-mouth on the streets.[1]

Ethicists tell us that the moral fiber of a society is gauged by how it treats its least-empowered members. That surely includes children. Scripture warns that God Almighty judges nations and individuals on their treatment of those least able to care for themselves: again, kids. Jesus expressed his loving concern for children on several occasions, cautioning that it's better to be drowned than to harm one of "these little ones."

And when God incarnated to become one of us, he did so as a helpless infant utterly dependent on the goodwill and care of adults.

---

1. See generally UNICEF, "State of the World's Children 2017," https://data.unicef.org/resources/state-worlds-children-2017-statistical-tables/; Human Rights Watch, "World Report 2017," https://www.hrw.org/world-report/2017; and National Center for Children in Poverty, "Child Poverty," http://www.nccp.org/topics/childpoverty.html.

## Rachel Weeping (Feast of the Holy Innocents)

My prayer is that we open our hearts to Rachel's tears as well as the tears of the world's suffering kids. Let's resolve to be better protectors of God's little ones. Let's stop Herod.

# Soul Journey (Epiphany)

"A cold coming we had of it
Just the worst time of year
For a journey, and such a long journey."

Thus begins T. S. Eliot's "The Journey of the Magi," a poetic meditation on the story of the Three Wise Men who travel from afar in search of the Christ Child. The Feast of Epiphany commemorates their pilgrimage.

The Epiphany story can be read in two ways: as a description of an actual historical event, or as an allegory of the soul's journey to God. Eliot's poem, written shortly after his own midlife conversion to Christianity, explores the story's allegorical side.

The poem is divided into three parts, corresponding to what Eliot sees as three spiritual stages through which God-seeking pilgrims pass: the hard journey to Bethlehem (searching for God), the encounter with the Christ child (finding God), and the return home (living in God).

The poem's speaker is one of the magi, now an old man reminiscing about the pilgrimage he and his two companions undertook years earlier.

In the poem's first part, the magus recalls the hardships encountered along the way: refractory camels, bad weather, unreliable guides, and filthy hostels. He remembers regretfully the pleasures he and his companions left behind.

> There were times we regretted
> The summer palaces on slopes, the terraces
> And the silken girls bringing sherbet.[1]

---

1. T. S. Eliot, *The Complete Poems and Plays, 1909–1950* (New York: Harcourt Brace Jovanovich, 1971), 68.

## Soul Journey (Epiphany)

Added to the physical hardships of the journey was the spiritual doubt that plagued the travelers with dark whispers that their trek "was all folly," a fool's errand, and that the wiser course would be to turn back to the comforts of home.

In the poem's second part, the seekers arrive at their destination. But, oddly, the magus doesn't describe the actual encounter with the infant Jesus. He simply recalls that he and his companions "arrived at evening, not a moment too soon."

Finally, in the poem's third part, the magus confesses that although he would gladly make the journey again, he isn't quite sure what to make of it. The Messianic birth heralded by the star also spelled a kind of death for him and his companions.

> We returned to our places, these Kingdoms,
> But no longer at ease here, in the old dispensation
> With an alien people clutching their gods.[2]

Many of us think of conversion as a one-off event that dispels all our religious doubts and suffuses us with uninterruptable joy.

But this is extremely rare. Much more commonly, conversion is a halting and laborious process so fraught with mental and spiritual uncertainty—although also offering moments of illuminating grace—that we're tempted at times to chuck the whole thing. Not only do we frequently feel as if we're groping in the dark, but we're also faced with the painful task of repudiating engrained behavior and beliefs that stand between us and God.

This is the initial stage of the soul journey, exemplified by the first part of Eliot's poem.

When we do make the breakthrough to faith—the second part of the poem as well as the second stage in soul journeying—we often find it difficult to pinpoint exactly when it occurred.

We awaken one day to discover that we've arrived at our destination: belief in God. The Spirit blows where it will, mysteriously, bafflingly. This explains why Eliot wisely refrains from having the magus say anything about his encounter with the infant Jesus. Words are inadequate to describe such an experience.

It's tempting to think this is the end of the journey for those of us who search for God. But it isn't. As Eliot says in the concluding third of

---

2. T. S. Eliot, *The Complete Poems and Plays, 1909–1950* (New York: Harcourt Brace Jovanovich, 1971), 68.

his poem, conversion is Janus-faced, pointing to birth on the one hand but death on the other.

Discovering God is a spiritual rejuvenation, but it also creates an unsettling sense of alienation from a culture—what Eliot calls the "old dispensation"—that genuflects before the idols of egoism, wealth, and power. Birth in God and living in God means an ongoing dying to worldliness, and dying is always a painful process.

Eliot's poem reminds us that soul journeying is more complex than we might imagine. But it's worth undertaking because it ultimately brings us to God. That's the meaning behind the story of the three magi. That's the gift of Epiphany.

# Becoming Saints (Lent)

In his autobiographical *The Seven Story Mountain*, Thomas Merton, one of the twentieth century's greatest spiritual writers, recalls a conversation with poet Robert Lax. The two friends were strolling in Greenwich Village shortly after Merton's conversion to Christianity when Lax threw this question at him: "What do you want to be, anyway?"

Taken by surprise, Merton lamely answered, "I don't know; I guess to be a good Catholic," whereupon Lax shot back, "What you should say is that you want to be a saint!" Bewildered, Merton asked, "How do you expect me to become a saint?" "By wanting to," Lax replied.[1]

The holy season of Lent begins on Ash Wednesday, the day in which Christians are reminded of the shortness of life ("dust you are, and to dust you shall return") and the consequent urgency of putting our spiritual houses in order ("repent, and believe in the Gospel"). The days that follow, right up to the Great Easter Vigil, are a period of time in which the faithful are called upon to fast, pray, and give alms.

All three are crucial. Fasting without prayer and almsgiving can morph into a New Year's-like resolution to lose a few pounds; giving alms minus the fasting and prayer can degenerate into casually scribbling a couple of checks; and prayer unaccompanied by fasting and almsgiving can easily become little more than talking to oneself.

These three traditional disciplines of Lent are so important because they're apprenticeships in sainthood. The desire for holiness ought to be with us throughout the entire year. But Lent is that season in the Christian calendar when we're called to double down on our efforts. Robert Lax was right. Our deepest, most heartfelt desire, even if we're not quite aware of it,

---

1. Thomas Merton, *The Seven Story Mountain* (Orlando: Harvest, 1999), 260.

is to grow ever more saintly, to enter ever more intimately into relationship with God.

All other desires are either expressions or perversions of this wellspring.

When we practice the three Lenten disciplines in a mindful rather than mechanical way, we begin, with God's help, to despoil ourselves of the egoistic conviction that we're the center of the universe. We open ourselves to the mystery that God is the circle whose center is everywhere and whose circumference is nowhere, and this leaves no room for our usual preoccupation with self. Such abandonment of ego is the resolute "heroic act," wrote Saint Thomas Aquinas, which leads to saintliness.

So prayer, almsgiving, and fasting are the first steps to becoming a saint. Prayer opens us up to communion with God, the only utterly real thing there is. Almsgiving bestows on us the blessed opportunity of sacrificing for others. Fasting gets us in the habit of disciplining our appetites for things that the world says are desirable—power, money, reputation, and so on—but which in fact exile us from God.

The Lenten disciplines do something else as well: they awaken a sense of profound gratitude in us by loosening the grip of pride. Pride is the great destroyer of gratitude because it refuses to recognize the value of anything that doesn't pleasure the rapacious ego. The proud person believes she deserves whatever she desires, and so nothing appears to her as gift. But for those who have tempered pride with the self-abandonment that comes from prayer, almsgiving, and fasting, everything is experienced as gift, and consequently everything is an occasion for gratitude.

The forty days of Lent echo the forty years the Hebrews wandered in the desert and the forty days Jesus resisted temptation in the wilderness. They invite us to venture into our inner deserts, our interior wildernesses, to face and subdue the ego that masquerades as our true self. They call us to leave the fleshpots of self-absorption so that we may discover our real identities: holy creatures made in the likeness of a lovingly self-emptying God.

Like Merton, we may be reluctant to embark on the Lenten path to saintliness. Doing so demands that we shed all our me-centered baggage along the way, and that's frightening. Or we may worry that our sins and imperfections so irreparably disqualify us for sainthood that shooting for it is presumptuous.

## Becoming Saints (Lent)

But the good news of Lent is this: both those who steel themselves to Aquinas's heroic resolve, and those who yearn for saintliness but think themselves unworthy of it, are already on the way.

# The True Myth (Easter)

When I was a teenager, I managed to snag a job in a secondhand bookstore by offering to work for books instead of cash. During my two years in that cramped, pell-mell, wonderfully Dickensian shop, I plowed my way through dozens of volumes. Few of them left deeper impressions than James Frazer's *The Golden Bough*, a wide-ranging study in comparative religion.

Frazer's denial that the theme of a slain and resurrected deity is unique to Christianity especially intrigued me. Many pre-Christian cultures, he pointed out, had similar tales. Myths about the Norse god Baldur, the Egyptian Osiris, and the Greek Dionysus are three of the best known.

I wasn't a particularly devout teen. But Frazer's claim that Jesus's death and resurrection was little more than the latest version of an ancient cross-cultural myth shook me. For several years following my reading of him, Frazer's debunking of the Christian story made for gloomy Easters.

My discomfort stemmed from my misunderstanding of what a myth is. I thought that "myth" was simply a synonym for "falsehood." I hadn't yet learned that the purpose of myth is to express fundamental truths about reality through the use of gripping imagery. Myths are narratives that move us for the same reason that good literature, poetry, art, or music do: they put words to our experiences of the deep-down pattern of existence. The language of myth evokes rather than literally describes. It illumines with flashes of insight.

Franciscan theologian Richard Rohr calls the fundamental pattern disclosed by myth the "great parabola." Everything, he says, rises and falls and rises again in a cosmic parabolic curve. Seasons come and go and return, creatures live, die, and are reborn through the transmission of genes, and stars come into being and eventually go nova, but their dust perdures. We notice this parabolic cycle of birth, dissolution, and rebirth everywhere.

## The True Myth (Easter)

So it's not surprising that stories about dying and rising gods can be found in more than one religious tradition.

Given this, the challenge for Christians is determining whether the death and resurrection commemorated during Holy Week really happened, or is cut from the same mythical cloth as tales about Baldur, Dionysus, and Osiris. Why, in other words, should the Christ-story be taken as anything more than just another mythic homage to the cosmic parabola?

It is impossible for a Christian to answer this question in a way that satisfies everyone. But the Anglican writer C. S. Lewis offered a line of reasoning that's worth thinking about, even though skeptics might dismiss it as a backwards reading of history. Lewis borrowed the idea from his longtime friend J. R. R. Tolkien, who was both an expert mythologist and a committed Roman Catholic.

Pre-Christian stories of dying and resurrected gods, suggested Lewis, are prefigurements of the Christ-event, born of vague, semi-articulable inklings of a coming seismic shift. It's as if the ancients sensed the earth tremble under their feet without quite understanding what it signified: the beginning of a parabolic swing which would climax in the death and resurrection of the Christ.

Lewis argued that this dim awareness of the coming Christ-event that made its way into stories of dying and rising deities was vitally necessary. It prepared the world to recognize and receive the one myth of a slain and resurrected God that is also factual. Pagan foreshadowings were previews of that staggering moment in history when what had been but a mythic dream became real.

So stories about Baldur, Dionysus, and Osiris, concluded Lewis, are "human myths." But the Christ-event is "God's myth." In pre-Christian days, God communicated the mystery of the great parabola "through the minds of poets, using such images as he found there." But in the death and resurrection of Christ, the communication is through "real things." The Christian story is the "true myth" that all prior human myths about dying and rising gods struggled mightily but haltingly to express.

It's this true myth, God's own myth, mirrored in the parabolic pattern of reality and inscribed on the human heart, which we joyfully and gratefully celebrate at Easter. The wide-eyed teenager devouring *The Golden Bough* all those years ago didn't get this. Five decades later, the man he became is beginning to.

# Sign of the Phoenix (Easter)

You don't have to be a professional historian to know that the full significance of legends is often only grasped in hindsight. Hints of meaningful patterns become more apparent with distance and perspective.

Take, for example, the legend of the phoenix, a mythical creature which, thanks to the Harry Potter series, has made something of a comeback in the popular imagination.

The phoenix is a marvelously plumed Arabian bird, about the size of an eagle, which periodically bursts into flame, is utterly consumed, and then rises again from its own ashes. For centuries, it's been a symbol of rebirth or resurrection.

We don't know quite when or where the phoenix legend originated—many scholars speculate that it comes from ancient Egypt—but the Greek poet Hesiod makes mention of the magical bird some 2,500 years ago. Other ancient authors, including Herodotus, Ovid, and Pliny, likewise refer to it. In their hands, the legend took on a variety of new details, as legends typically do when they're passed from one generation or culture to the next.

What remained constant, though, was the theme of rebirth.

Not surprisingly, early Christians such as Saint Clement, Saint Cyril of Alexandria, and Saint Ambrose saw the phoenix as a symbol of both the resurrected Christ and the promised postmortem resurrection of humans. The second-century Christian apologist Tertullian invoked the legend when he rhetorically asked: "Can it be that humans will die once and for all, while Arabian birds are assured of a resurrection?"

Taken by itself, the myth of the phoenix is fascinating enough. But it becomes even more intriguing when one looks back at the course of history and realizes that it's part of a larger pattern. Legends abound of mythical creatures, humans, and even gods who die only to be reborn. The motif is apparent in stories about Osiris, Ishtar, Persephone, Adonis, Bacchus, and

## Sign of the Phoenix (Easter)

Baldur. Comparative mythologist Joseph Campbell convincingly argues that the death-rebirth theme is one of the most common in folklore, epics, and even fairy tales.

Like a golden thread, then, the theme of rising from the ashes of death runs throughout the world's oldest and deepest myths, forever finding ways to express itself anew (as in the Harry Potter books).

Now, there are two ways to explain this pattern. The first is to presume that it's nothing more than a psychological coping mechanism to deal with the death fear that's always haunted humans, and that cultural drift, the slow process by which mythical motifs migrate from one culture to another, has scattered traces of the death-rebirth story throughout the world.

According to this way of thinking, the resurrection of Jesus Christ is simply the most recent expression of the mythical pattern. The Christ story is the latest retelling of a psycho-historical motif.

But what if the world's myths of death and rebirth, including that of the phoenix, are historical and cultural stabs at expressing a great truth about reality that, until two thousand years ago, was only vaguely intuited and dimly understood? What if it's the case that such myths are all imaginative efforts to give voice to a hardwired realization, one that's taken centuries to reach full consciousness, that death is not the final destiny of humanity—nor, for that matter, of creation itself?

If we take this possibility seriously, we can certainly agree with those who say that the resurrection of Jesus Christ is the most recent expression of an ancient mythical pattern. But we can also conclude that it's a "true myth," a myth become fact, poetry made real, an event whose inevitability was expressed again and again in the various cultural manifestations of the death-rebirth motif.

In this view, earlier resurrection myths are foretellings that point to the great turning-point truth of Christ's resurrection, the cosmic renewal commemorated and celebrated at Easter.

When asked for proof of his divinity, Jesus offered the "sign of Jonah," meaning that just as the prophet Jonah had emerged after three days in the whale's belly, the Messiah would resurrect after three days in the tomb.

He could just as easily have offered the "sign of the phoenix."

# Light and Darkness
# (Feast of the Transfiguration)

We live in a chiaroscuro world, you and I, where light and darkness forever dance with one another. Sometimes light leads, sometimes darkness.

Each year on August 6, the Christian world observes the Feast of the Transfiguration, traditionally a celebration of light. The event it commemorates is recorded in three of the Gospels.

Jesus takes his closest disciples, Peter, John and James, to a mountaintop. Once there, a miracle occurs. Jesus suddenly becomes "radiant," emitting a white light that blinds and frightens his companions. He blazes forth "like the sun" and even his clothes appear "dazzling white, as no one on earth could bleach them." And in the midst of this laser show, the voice of God thunders, "This is my Son. Listen to him!"

What happened two thousand years ago on that mountain was a revelatory explosion of divine light. In a flash brighter than ten suns, in an eruption of Godstuff as intense as a burst of pure white light, the Eternal lightning-bolted to earth. It's as if all the energy that goodness and truth offer went nova in the person of this strange man from Galilee.

Fast-forward from first-century Palestine to mid-twentieth century Asia. August 6, 1945, to be precise. At 8:15 in the morning on that Feast of the Transfiguration, another nova of light and energy occurred, this time over a Japanese city named Hiroshima. The nuclear bomb dropped by the "Enola Gay" exploded about two thousand feet above the earth's surface.

The temperature of the atomic burst, one million degrees Celsius, set the atmosphere on fire, birthing the horrible ball of light that survivors said was also brighter than ten suns. Between 80 and 140,000 people were vaporized in an instant, and another 100,000 horribly burned.

## Light and Darkness (Feast of the Transfiguration)

There was no voice from heaven at this explosion of light. But something that more than fit the occasion had been uttered two weeks earlier when the world's first atomic bomb was tested at Trinity, New Mexico. Stunned by the unimaginable destructiveness of the explosion, the physicist J. Robert Oppenheimer despairingly recalled a passage from the Hindu scripture *Bhagavad Gita*: "Now I am become death, the destroyer of worlds."

The chiaroscuro of existence, horribly captured in a single day. The vitality-filled light of transfiguration on the one hand, and its netherworld doppelganger, the death-dealing flash of nuclear holocaust, on the other. "This is my Son!" side-by-side with "I am become death!" How can we not be haunted by such a nightmarish coupling?

I hesitate to draw lessons here, lest I trivialize either the glory of the transfiguration or the irredeemable evil of the bomb. But perhaps two thoughts can be ventured.

The first is that darkness can sometimes masquerade as light. Our ancestors were well aware of what we sophisticated moderns have chosen to forget: the Evil One is a liar and a deceiver. Wickedness often roams the world openly like a roaring lion, but more often it pretends to be something other than it is. The blinding blast of light over Hiroshima, darkness's mocking impersonation of Transfigurative light, reminds us of this tragic truth.

Here's the second lesson. The dance of light and darkness is inescapable, and it takes only a subtle shift in the rhythm of time for the two to change positions. Their dance is all around us, but it's in us, too. We forever minuet with a darkness that threatens to take the lead and pivot us toward destruction. This is the human condition, and if we try to sugarcoat it with comfortable pietisms, we risk being ravished by the darkness, especially when it disguises itself as light.

Reality isn't one or the other, light or darkness. It's both. No one intuited this coexistence better than the apostle John, who proclaimed at the very beginning of his Gospel, "the light shines in the darkness, but the darkness doesn't understand it." And this chiaroscuro world in which we dwell makes human existence a perpetual seesawing between hope and despair, joy and sorrow, resilience and surrender, acceptance and defiance, faith and doubt, good and evil. It's always been this way.

After Hiroshima, we know this (or at least we should know it) in our very bones. After Hiroshima, the Feast of the Transfiguration is no longer only a joyful celebration of light. It's also a somber reminder of darkness.

www.ingramcontent.com/pod-product-compliance
Lightning Source LLC
Chambersburg PA
CBHW031357230426
43670CB00006B/570